# Make:

D1230828

# Making Simple
# ROBOTS
## 2nd Edition

## KATHY CECERI

# Make:
# Making Simple Robots, 2nd Edition

By Kathy Ceceri

Copyright © 2022 Kathy Ceceri. All rights reserved.

Published by Make Community, LLC
150 Todd Road, Suite 100, Santa Rosa, CA 95407

*Make:* books may be purchased for educational, business, or sales promotional use.
Online editions are also available for most titles.
For more information, contact our corporate/institutional sales department:
800-998-9938

**Publisher:** Dale Dougherty
**Editor:** Michelle Lowman
**Copy Editor:** Sophia Smith
**Creative Direction/Design:** Juliann Brown
**Photography:** Kathy Ceceri
**Illustrations:** Juliann Brown

2015 First Edition
Revision History for the First Edition
05/06/2022

See www.oreilly.com/catalog/errata.csp?isbn=9781680457308 for release details.

*Make:*, Maker Shed, and Maker Faire are registered trademarks of Make Community, LLC. The Make: Community logo is a trademark of Make Community, LLC. *Making Simple Robots, 2nd Edition* and related trade dress are trademarks of Make Community, LLC. Many of the designations used by manufacturers and sellers to distinguish their products are claimed as trademarks. Where those designations appear in this book, and Make Community, LLC was aware of a trademark claim, the designations have been printed in caps or initial caps. While the publisher and the authors have made good faith efforts to ensure that the information and instructions contained in this work are accurate, the publisher and the authors disclaim all responsibility for errors or omissions, including without limitation responsibility for damages resulting from the use of or reliance on this work. Use of the information and instructions contained in this work is at your own risk. If any code samples or other technology this work contains or describes are subject to open source licenses or the intellectual property rights of others, it is your responsibility to ensure that your use thereof complies with such licenses and/or rights.

978-1-68045-730-8

## O'Reilly Online Learning

For more than 40 years, www.oreilly.com has provided technology and business training, knowledge, and insight to help companies succeed.

Our unique network of experts and innovators share their knowledge and expertise through books, articles, conferences, and our online learning platform. O'Reilly's online learning platform gives you on-demand access to live training courses, in-depth learning paths, interactive coding environments, and a vast collection of text and video from O'Reilly and 200+ other publishers. For more information, please visit www.oreilly.com.

## How to Contact Us:

Please address comments and questions concerning this book to the publisher:

**Make: Community**

150 Todd Road, Suite 100, Santa Rosa, CA 95407

You can also send comments and questions to us by email at books@make.co.

Make: Community is a growing, global association of makers who are shaping the future of education and democratizing innovation. Through *Make:* magazine, and 200+ annual Maker Faires, *Make:* books, and more, we share the know-how of makers and promote the practice of making in schools, libraries, and homes.

To learn more about *Make:* visit us at make.co.

# #1

# Robots Inspired by Nature.......................1

# #5

# Making Robots Playful.........................150

# Preface
## TROUBLESHOOTING FOR SUCCESS

In this book, I introduce you to the most valuable skill a robot builder (or any kind of inventor) can have.

It isn't knowing how to work with power tools, soldering irons, or laser cutters. Those skills are useful when you're building more complicated robots – but you won't need them to make any of the robots in this book.

And it's not being able to write computer programs, or create 2D and 3D art — although you'll get to do both as you try out the projects in these pages.

So what's the super-important skill every robot-maker needs?

It's knowing how to troubleshoot!

*Troubleshooting* is a way to figure out why your project isn't working and how to fix it. It means:
- Going back through each step you followed, one by one.
- Looking for clues that could point to what went wrong.
- Coming up with ideas that might fix the problem.
- Keep trying different ideas until you find the right one.

Troubleshooting is the reason why people like engineers, programmers, designers, and artists don't just give up and walk away as soon as things go ka-blooey.

It's how anyone can take a failure and – with a little luck – turn it into a success. (A lot of the time, at least.)

If that sounds tough, it is! Learning how to troubleshoot can be hard for beginners, especially if you've never tried to fix anything yourself before. Just like any new skill, it takes practice to get good at it.

It might help to think about a time when you didn't know how to do something that's really easy now, like writing your name, or riding a bike. Maybe you figured it out quickly. But chances are, you needed a little help and encouragement to get started. And the more you practiced, the better you got. Doing it over and over helped you build up the muscles in your hand that let you hold a pen straight, or the muscles in your legs that help you pump the pedals.

When you practice troubleshooting, you build up your persistence muscles. They help you stop feeling frustrated and keep going, until you figure out whether or not your problem can be solved.

Of course, not every idea works out. Sometimes even the best robot-builders have to give up and try something else. The family behind Beatty Robotics, Camille and Genevieve Beatty and their dad Robert (an engineer and author of the best-selling Serafina adventure series), began fooling around with robot kits when the sisters were only 9 and 11. They quickly filled a container with burned-up electronics and broken tool bits that they jokingly called the "Box of Shame." But they didn't let their failures slow them down. With every project, they learned a little bit more and got a little bit better. And just a couple of years later, they were building working models of space rovers for science museums all around the world.

How can you learn to be persistent, like the Beatty family? Here are some tips that may help you push through the tough spots:

- Give yourself plenty of time to figure out any steps that may give you trouble.
- Get extra supplies, in case something breaks or is defective.
- Keep an eye out for inspiring people and projects at places like robot competitions, science festivals, museums, and Maker Faires.
- To improve your skills, look for classes, camps, or clubs where teachers and other experts can guide you as you work.
- Check out websites like Make.co, Instructables.com, and ScienceBuddies.org, and books like the one you're reading now to get

ideas and possible answers to problems you can't figure out.

- Share the skills you develop with other people. Teaching is a great way to learn new things yourself!
- Finally, think about creating your own "box of shame." It may come in handy when you need a spare part. And it will remind you how far you've come when you troubleshoot your way to a successful project!

Good luck! If you have questions, comments, or suggestions about this book, feel free to contact me. I'd love to hear about your adventures making simple robots!

Kathy Ceceri
kathyceceri.com

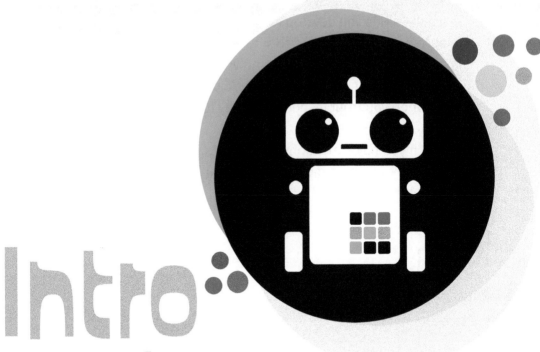

# Intro

## MAKING SIMPLE ROBOT PROTOTYPES FROM EVERYDAY STUFF

# ROBOTS ARE GETTING SIMPLER ALL THE TIME.

If that sounds backwards, think about this: The average smartphone is faster and holds more information than the biggest computer 50 years ago!

Not only that, but a smartphone knows what's going on around it, thanks to its built-in touch sensor, tilt sensor, compass, and GPS. It can see and hear with its camera and microphone, talk back with its speaker, and display words and pictures on its screen. It can even connect with other devices over phone networks or the internet, anywhere in the world.

Now imagine fitting all that technology into a tiny robot!

The same miniature electronics used in smartphones make even simple robots super powerful. And since they don't need a lot of space for their brains, robot bodies can be made out of soft materials like flexible plastic, rubbery skin, and even paper and fabric. Some robots don't even need brains! That makes them cheap and easy to build and replace.

All of this is great news for robot beginners. *Making Simple Robots* will show you how to use ordinary arts and crafts materials and skills you already have to build working models that are surprisingly close to the real thing — no lab or fancy equipment needed!

Even the most basic projects in *Making Simple Robots* introduce you to different aspects of robotics. Some can be done in one sitting. Others can easily be broken down into steps that can be completed over a few sessions. It's also OK if you've never worked with electronics or computer programming. Everything you need to know is described in detail, with step-by-step pictures to show you the way.

# WHAT IS A SIMPLE ROBOT?

When we talk about robots, we generally mean machines that can do three things: *sense*, *think*, and *act*. A robot can:

- use sensors to tell what's happening in the space around it,
- use its computer brain to react to that information, based on its programming,
- move around, flash lights, play music or alarms, or generally do anything that affects the physical world.

How can you tell if something is a robot or just an ordinary machine? Here's an example: A vacuum turns on when you flip a switch. But it will sit in one spot forever unless you grab the handle and start pushing it over the carpet. If you bang it into a chair leg (or a dog's tail), it doesn't change anything about the way it runs — it goes where you steer it.

A Roomba, on the other hand, is a computerized vacuum. It can be programmed to turn itself on at certain times. And when it bumps into something, it "learns" to go around it. You may think of a Roomba as a glorified floor sweeper, but it's actually a full-fledged robot.

You may find other "robots" around your home or neighborhood too. An automatic garage door with sensors that tell it to stop if something's in the way also counts as a robot. So does a clothes dryer that stops tumbling when its moisture sensor detects that the towels are done.

But not every robot needs a brain and sensors! Even "dumb" machines can behave like they're intelligent. Some robots don't even use a motor or electrical power.

In this book, you'll find all robot projects at all levels. There are robots that don't use any electronics at all, some that run on motors and batteries, and some that are programmable using miniature computers that fit on a board and free, easy-to-learn software. There are even activities that show you how to create virtual robots that exist only on the computer screen. But no matter how basic they are, all the projects were inspired by actual robots developed by researchers, scientists, or robot fans around the world.

And they're all simple, because they're all made from everyday stuff!

# What Is the Design Thinking Process?

Before robotics researchers build a new robot, they create a prototype. A prototype is a model that looks and/or acts like the final version, but is usually much smaller and simpler to make. Robot laboratories use prototypes to test out their ideas and identify any problems before they build the real thing. That way, they can make changes quickly and cheaply, and test them out again.

This practice of prototyping, testing, and improving over and over is called iteration. It's part of the Design Thinking Process. Also known as the "Engineering Design Process" and other names, it's a series of steps that helps you turn an idea into a working prototype. There are different versions, but here's mine:

## STEP 1:
**LIST YOUR REQUIREMENTS:** What do you want your robot to do? What problem do you want it to solve, or challenge do you want it to meet? If you are creating a project to help other people, make sure you get their input at every stage!

## STEP 2:
**PLAN YOUR PROJECT:** Brainstorm ideas to try, and then narrow it down to the one(s) you think will work best. Make sure you take into account any limits on materials, tools, and time.

## STEP 3:
**STOP, REVIEW, AND GET FEEDBACK:** Before you begin building, go back over your plans one more time. If you've got questions, now's the time to look for expert advice.

## STEP 4:

**BUILD YOUR PROTOTYPE — AND DOCUMENT WHAT YOU DO:** As you work, keep a record of what you use. Write down the instructions for your project, and make notes where you made changes. Take photos and videos so you can watch your progress. Engineers learn to record everything they do, from the very beginning of a project. They draw sketches and write notes in a bound notebook with the pages sewn in, and they date every page. That way, they have proof that the ideas they came up with are their own.

## STEP 5:

**TEST YOUR DESIGN:** Once you've got your prototype, it's time to test it out. Does it work the way you expected? If not, take note of the details and move on to the next step.

## STEP 6:

**TROUBLESHOOT AND REFINE:** Read "**Troubleshooting for Success**" on page viii to find out why this is the most important skill you may ever learn. Every time you go over a project and discover what went wrong, or what could be improved, you become a better maker. And developing the patience to keep going when things are going wrong will make life a lot more enjoyable. There's no better feeling than figuring out where the problem is, and how to fix it!

Ready? Then it's time to start *Making Simple Robots*!

# Suggested Supply List

This master list includes the suggested supplies for all the projects in this book, including basic and advanced versions. Using scrap and recycled materials and things from your supply closet, you can probably do all the projects in the book for roughly $50. To see exactly what is required for each individual project, go to the project instructions. And if you don't have any of the items on this list, don't worry! You can substitute something you do have on hand for many of the suggested materials. That's how new robot designs are born!

**ELECTRONICS AND CIRCUIT-BUILDING SUPPLIES** (Figure Ⓐ)
- Computer
  - USB ports required for some projects
  - Internet access, or offline versions of:
    - Scratch 3
    - MakeCode for micro:bit
- micro:bit v2 (version 2) microcontroller board
  - Version 1 (v1) will also work, but without sound
  - micro:bit Go kit comes with:
    - micro:bit microcontroller board
    - Short USB cable
    - AAA battery pack
    - AAA batteries
    - Punch-out cardboard holder to attach the battery pack to the board

> **NOTE:** Other microcontroller boards will work as well, including the Adafruit Circuit Playground Express.

- USB data cable with a USB micro B plug and an end that fits your computer
- 1 or 2 micro (9g) servo motors (positional, not continuous)

- 2 servo horns; 1 should have 2 long arms
- 3 alligator clip-to-male jumper wires in different colors (preferably red, black or brown, and yellow or orange to match the servo wires)

- Optional:
  - Extra-long USB data cable
  - Male-to-female jumper wires
  - AA battery pack with JST connection, 2 AA batteries, and on/off switch

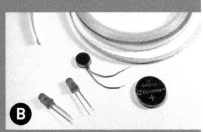

- Printer (to print out templates)
- 2 LEDs with medium to long wire leads (they should be the same color) (Figure B)
- 2 coin batteries 3V (CR2032 or similar)
- Mini 3V (3 volt) vibrating disk motor

- Conductive copper foil or nylon tape with conductive glue (aluminum foil tape used for heating ducts can also be made to work)
- Optional tools:
  - Wire stripper
  - 3D Printer

## CRAFTS MATERIALS AND SEWING, HARDWARE, OFFICE AND HOUSEHOLD SUPPLIES (Figure C)

- **Art and Household Supplies**
  - Googly eyes (1 large, several small)
  - Pipe cleaners
  - 4 or more beads with large holes, such as pony beads
  - Twist ties (re-used, or a roll of garden twist tie wire)

- 2 paper cups or other small, lightweight recycled containers or cardboard boxes
- 12 disposable drinking straws (such as sturdy paper straws)
- Crayola Model Magic modeling compound, or other rubbery, self-drying material, white or colored to match your skin
- Clay modeling tools, or kitchen utensils such as:
  - Unsharpened pencil with clean eraser
  - Toothpicks
  - Craft sticks
  - Disposable forks, knives, and spoons
- 3 twisting balloons and a balloon hand pump

- **Paper**
  - Index card
  - Copy paper
  - Cardstock (heavy printable paper)
  - Construction paper
  - Thin stiff cardboard
  - Corrugated cardboard scraps
  - Drawing paper or pad

- **Tape and Glue**
  - Clear tape
  - Electrical tape
  - Masking tape
  - Double-sided scrapbooking tape or adhesive dots
  - Optional:
    - Hot glue gun
    - Duct tape

- **School/Office Supplies**
  - Pen or marker
  - Washable markers
  - Scissors

- Optional: craft knife or mini utility knife
- Ruler
- Sharp pencil (for poking holes as well as writing)
- Optional: ball point pen or bamboo skewer
- 6 rubber bands, about 7 inches long
- 6 small thin rubber bands (such as ponytail or bracelet bands)
- Paper clips
- Small (3/4 inch) binder clip
- Optional: Mouse pad

- **Hardware**
  - Flexible vinyl tubing, 1/4-inch (15 cm) inside diameter

- **Sewing**
  - 1 by 2 feet (30 by 60 centimeters) fabric that's easy to work with, such as felt, fleece, denim, or burlap
  - Felt, two or more colors
    - (Optional) peel-and-stick felt
  - Embroidery yarn (also called craft yarn, less glossy than embroidery floss)
  - Wide needle with an eye large enough for a full strand of embroidery yarn, such as a tapestry needle (with a rounded point) or embroidery needle (with a sharp point)
  - Fiberfill stuffing
  - Peel-and-stick fabric adhesive sheets (the no-iron type)
  - Peel-and-stick Velcro tape or dots to attach the battery pack to the fabric

**Get your companion starter pack** with all the electronics you'll need and then some for the projects in *Making Simple Robots, 2nd Edition* including the micro:bit v.2! Grab yours at makershed.com/simplerobotpack.

# #1
# ROBOTS INSPIRED BY NATURE

Explore **soft robotics** with models that take after living things!

Do you ever think about what robots are made of? A robot's body needs to fit its job. And since robots can do so many different things, scientists are always looking for ways to create bodies that will help the robot do what it needs to do!

In old science fiction movies, robots were always big, heavy, and blocky. To show off how powerful they were, their bodies were made of metal. Even human-shaped robots looked kind of like factory machinery. In the real world, household robots like robo-vacuums and robotic toys are usually made of plastic. Their bodies are smaller and lighter, but still strong and hard to damage.

However, one branch of robotics is focused on a different way of building robots. **Soft robots** can bend, stretch, and squeeze themselves through tight spots, just like a cat or an octopus. In fact, many soft robots are **biomimetic,** which means they're modeled after living things. Biomimetic robots copy the way people and animals walk, crawl, swim, or fly. Since they're based upon millions of years of evolution, they can also be more efficient than other robot designs. They may require less power and less programming than hard-bodied, machine-like robots to get where they want to go.

Soft robots are also more **compliant** — a robotics term meaning they are safe to use around people and delicate things. If your supermarket tried to use a big metal robot arm to pack groceries, chances are it would end up smushing the bananas and cracking the eggs. But if you gave the job to a compliant robot hand, such as the fin gripper claw in this chapter, it would gently close around each object.

Let's start our robot adventures by creating some soft robotic prototypes inspired by nature. The projects in this chapter are made with everyday materials like stiff paper and twisty balloons. Paper makes a good material for building robot models because it can be stiff enough to stand up, yet soft enough to act like a spring when folded. Balloons are incredibly light — and when they're filled with air, they can also be incredibly strong.

You may be surprised how much these super-simple designs behave like the real thing!

# Project: Make a Paper Walking Robot Dog

## CREATE A GRAVITY-POWERED QUADRUPED FROM AN INDEX CARD

For this project, you'll build a robot that moves without any computers or sensors to guide it. In fact, this version is so basic, it doesn't even need a motor! Instead, it is powered by the pull of gravity. This style of motion is known as **passive dynamic** walking.

Scientists used to think that people and animals relied on their brains to control the way they walked and keep their balance. But it turns out that a lot of that control is taken care of by the legs themselves — an example of a smart body in action! The legs swing back and forth and shift the weight of the body from side to side. Once they get started, the legs keep going forward until the brain tells them to stop. It's an efficient and stable system, which is why robotics engineers have borrowed it to use in walking robots.

Most passive dynamic walkers are bipeds and walk on two legs. When they move, they shift all their weight to one leg, and let the other leg swing forward. Then they shift their weight the other way to allow the other foot to take a step. (Check out my book *BOTS!* to see how to make a two-legged version.)

However, some robotics labs have tried making passive dynamic walkers with three, four, or even more legs! The extra legs help with balance, but they also make the pattern of walking much more complicated. When a dog walks along, it only picks up one foot at a time. A cheetah or a race horse can trot with two feet always on the ground at the same time, or gallop with just one foot touching down as it speeds by. Trying to get a four-legged robot to move in a realistic way is a big problem scientists are still trying to solve.

One robot dog called Spot, made by Boston Dynamics, has a gait (or pattern of walking) that's so real, it's spooky. Spot's legs bend the same way real dog legs bend. And with its sensors and programming, Spot is good at getting itself back up if it tumbles over on its side. The Walking Robot Dog you will be making, on the other hand, doesn't even have knees, so its legs don't bend. But it does move one front foot and then the other in a slow, steady rhythm as it makes its way downhill. It also has a long skinny neck and a small head, like Spot. The head and tail help keep it balanced. Even though it isn't as advanced as Spot, it's still pretty good at not falling over.

However, there is one engineering challenge you'll have to solve: The Walking Paper Robot Dog has no feet. That means it has very little traction to keep it from sliding downhill. (Think about how the somewhat sticky rubber on your sneakers, or a dog's rough paw pads, help the feet grip the floor.) You may need to find or add a bumpy or sticky texture to your test ramp, or directly to the ends of your robot's legs!

## WHAT TO EXPECT
- **Time Needed:** Less than 1 hour
- **Cost:** Less than $1
- **Difficulty:** Easy
- **Safety Issues:** None

## SKILLS USED
Folding, measuring (or eyeballing measurements), cutting along lines

## SUPPLIES
**FOR THE ROBOT:**
- Index card, cardstock, or construction paper (get two sheets if you're using it for the ramp as well); 4 inches by 6 inches is a good size
- Pen, pencil, or marker
- Scissors
- Ruler
- Tape
- Optional: 2 paper clips

**FOR THE TEST RAMP:**
- A board or other large flat object, about a foot long
- Something to prop up the ramp, such as a pile of books
- Optional: a covering such as construction paper, rough cardboard, or a rubbery mouse pad to give the ramp a little traction

## INSTRUCTIONS
1. To start, look at the template to get an idea of how your robot dog will look, and then draw your own fold and cut lines. First, measure the length of the card or heavy paper you are using. Divide the length into three, and mark each section on the card. In other words, if your card is 4 inches by 6 inches, make marks along the longer side at 2 inches and 4 inches.

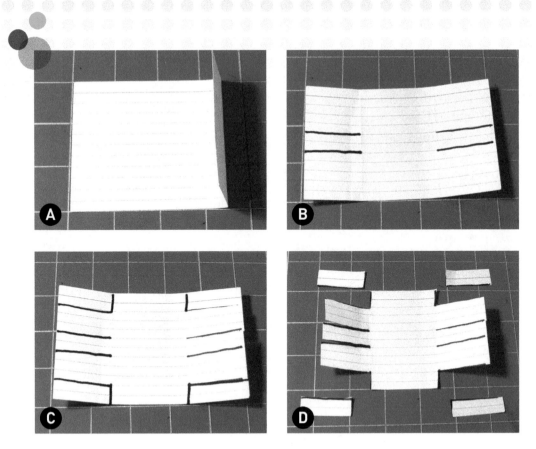

2. To make the front and back leg sections, fold up the ends of the card (Figure **A**). Check that the sections are equal by flipping the card over and standing it up on its legs like a table. Unfold.

3. To make the head and tail: mark a narrow strip down the middle of the front and back sections you just made, going from the fold to the edge of the paper (Figure **B**). (If there are lines on the index card, use them to guide you.)

4. To make the front legs, draw a line on either side of the front end. Repeat on the other end of the card to make the back legs (Figure **C**).

5. To make a wide stomach (which helps the dog rock side to side as it walks), cut off the bit that is left between the legs and the edge of the card (Figure **D**).

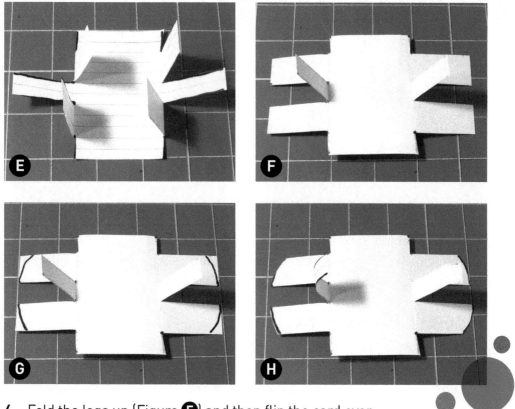

6. Fold the legs up (Figure **E**) and then flip the card over.

7. Bend the head and tail up (Figure **F**). To help the dog rock side to side and lift its feet to walk, round off the feet like a rocking chair. Draw a curve on each foot, starting at the inside corner and going up a little ways along the side of the card (Figure **G**). Cut along the lines. Test that the legs are still even and trim them if they are not.

8. Finish the head by folding down a little at the tip. Finish the tail by curling it around a pen (Figure **H**).

9. To get the dog to walk, place it at the top of the ramp. Tilt the ramp until the dog starts to move. You can get it going by tapping on one side of its belly (Figure **I**).

## TROUBLESHOOTING TIPS

If it doesn't work, what could be the problem? Look at:

- **Balance:** Are the front and back legs the same length?
- **Legs:** Is the fold connecting them to the body sharp enough to allow them to move?
- **Feet:** Are they curved evenly?
- **Rocking:** Does the dog tilt from side to side as it moves? If not, try adding a little weight by taping a paperclip underneath each side.
- **Body:** Is it stiff enough? If not, make it thicker with tape, or add another layer of paper.
- **Ramp:** Is it tilted too little or too much? Is it too slippery?

## GO BEYOND

- Can you design a two-legged walker that doesn't need back legs? How will it balance? How will its legs swing back and forth? (Think about different kinds of two-legged walkers from real life, such as birds, or their cousins the dinosaurs.)
- Take a look at some early passive dynamic walkers from Cornell University: ruina.tam.cornell.edu/research/topics/robots.

# Project: Make a Cardstock Fin Gripper Claw

**THE TAIL OF A FISH IS THE MODEL FOR A ROBOT HAND
THAT BENDS AROUND THE SHAPE IT GRABS!**

Like robot legs, robot arms (also called *effectors*) are something scientists find very challenging to design. Human hands are filled with nerves, muscles, tendons, bones, and joints to help them move where and how we want them to. Some robot hands use the same structure as human hands, such as cables that act like our tendons do, pulling the fingers so they curl and straighten.

But many robot arms look to other kinds of living things for inspiration. Octopus tentacles are one popular option. The German robotics company Festo makes an octopus-style arm that wraps itself all the way around an object. It even has suction cups to help it hold on.

Festo makes several biomimetic robot parts. Its BionicSoftArm was inspired by the way an elephant uses its long, bendy trunk to pick up objects. You can attach different kinds of grippers to Festo's arm — including one that's designed to work like the tail fin of a fish! A fin gripper "finger" looks like a triangle-shaped ladder. When you press in one side, or squeeze one corner of the base, it curls in that direction. The "rungs" of the ladder keep the fin gripper more or less in the same pointy triangle shape.

On a fish, this kind of tail can push against the pressure of the water with more force. On a robot hand, two or more fin gripper fingers can be put together to make a claw that curls around objects without crushing them.

This paper version of a fin gripper finger is based on a paper model Festo offers for students, but it's been simplified to use only one strip of paper. You can create a fin gripper claw by connecting two or more fin grippers to a "wrist." When you pull the fingers in, they press up against whatever you want them to grab and hold it tight.

## WHAT TO EXPECT
- **Time Needed:** 1 hour
- **Cost:** Less than $1
- **Difficulty:** Easy
- **Safety Issues:** Be careful when poking holes through the cardstock

## SKILLS USED
Folding, measuring, cutting along lines, poking holes safely

## SUPPLIES
- 2 fin gripper finger templates, or two strips of cardstock or other heavy paper or thin cardboard, about 11 inches by 1 1/2 inches
- Templates for the tube, tube bottom, and springy base, or three pieces of cardstock in these sizes:
  - 1 skinny strip, 1 1/2 inch by 11 inches wide
  - 1 fat strip, 4 inch by 11 inches wide
  - 1 circle 3 1/2 inches across, with 1-inch tabs on opposite sides.
- Disposable drinking straw
- Scissors
- Sharp pencil
- Tape

## TEMPLATES

- **Green:** Fin Gripper Fingers
- **Pink:** Springy Base
- **Yellow:** Tube Sides
- **Blue:** Tube Bottom

(Downloadable templates: makezine.com/go/simple-robot-templates)

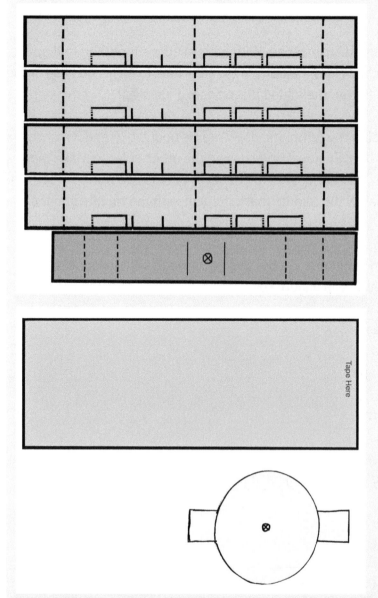

Tape Here

*Each template should be enlarged to fit on a letter-sized piece of cardstock.*

## NOTES
- Dotted lines = fold
- Solid lines = cut
- You can make your gripper any size, as long as the proportions are similar — in other words, keep the shape about the same.

## INSTRUCTIONS

1. Fold the cardboard strip in half. With bottom edges together, fold up about 1 1/4 inches from the bottom to make tabs to form the base of the triangle. Then flatten the folded piece again (Figure **A**).

2. If you're not using the template, draw marks about 1, 2, and 3 inches above the fold line. Flip over and copy on the other side. To make the "rungs" of the "ladder," draw a tab about 1/4 inch wide from the bottom mark to just below the middle mark. Repeat with the middle and top marks.

3. For the bottom rung only, cut out the tab through both layers of the folded cardboard strip (Figure **B**).

4. To form the base of the triangle, spread the sides apart (Figure **C**). Fold both base tabs in toward the middle. Overlap so that the base is about 2 inches wide. Tape the base tabs together (Figure **D**).

5. Fold the bottom rung tabs in. They should overlap, but don't tape them yet (Figure **E**).

6. Cut the middle and top rungs and fold them in (Figure **F**).

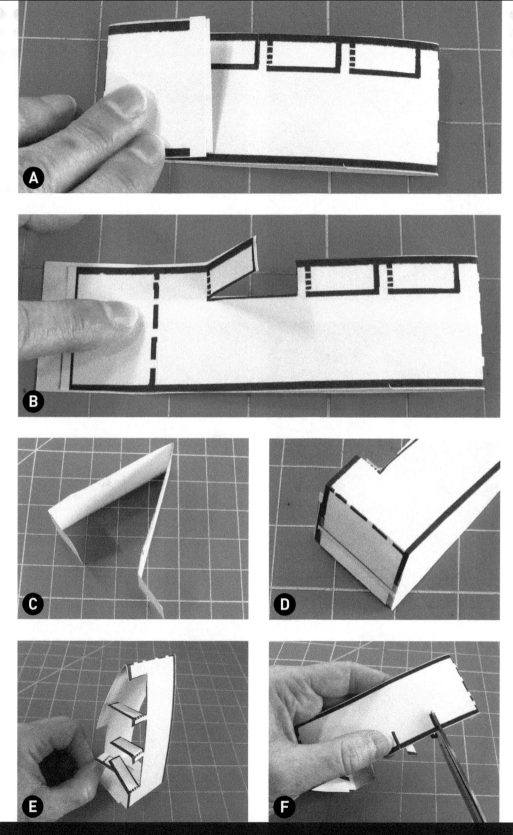

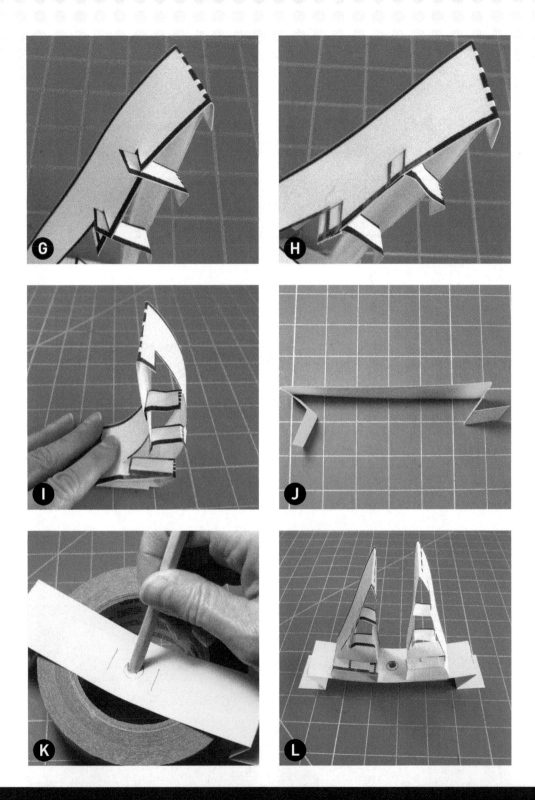

7. On the opposite side, cut slots at the middle and top marks. Insert the middle and top rungs through the slots (Figure **G**). Fold down the extra bit and tape closed. It's okay if the sides of the triangle are pulled in a little (Figure **H**).

8. For the bottom rung, tape the overlapped ends together. Reinforce the rung with extra tape.

9. To test the fin gripper finger, squeeze one corner of the base to make the gripper curl in that direction (Figure **I**). If it doesn't work, check that the rungs are not bending when the fin curves. You can reinforce them by wrapping them with tape. Also, make sure the tabs are held in place tightly. Add extra tape if necessary.

10. Repeat to make a second fin gripper.

11. To make a claw, start with the springy base to hold the fin gripper "fingers." Use the template, or cut a strip of cardstock about 1 1/2 inches wide and 10 inches long. Fold each end in about an inch. Then flip the strip over and fold the folded end in again the same way. This creates accordion (Z-shaped) "springs" at the ends (Figure **J**).

12. If you don't use the template, mark the middle of the strip, springs facing down. Then make marks on either side of the center mark, about half an inch away.

13. Take a sharp pencil and poke a hole in the center (Figure **K**).

    **TIP:** To hold the strip steady, it helps to rest it on top of a roll of masking tape or a stack of corrugated cardboard.

14. Tape the fingers onto the strip at the outer marks, with the cross pieces (the ladder rungs) facing you (Figure **L**).

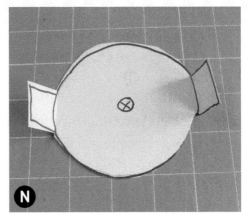

**15.** To make the "wrist," use the template or cut a strip of cardstock about 4 inches wide and 11 inches long. Tape the short ends together to make a tube (Figure **M**).

**16.** Cut out the template for the bottom of the tube, including the tabs (they look like ears), or trace around the tube on another piece of cardstock and draw two tabs on opposite sides, about 1 square inch (Figure **N**).

**17.** Fold the tabs up. Use the pencil to poke a hole in the center of the bottom, the same way you did with the strip. Tape the bottom onto the tube, with one tab over the tube's seam (Figure **O**).

**18.** Take a paper straw and cut three snips around one end to create tabs. Fold the tabs back like the petals of a flower (Figure **P**).

**19.** Insert the straw through the hole in the springy base strip so the tabs rest on top, between the fin gripper fingers. Tape the straw tabs to the strip to hold the straw in place (Figure **Q**).

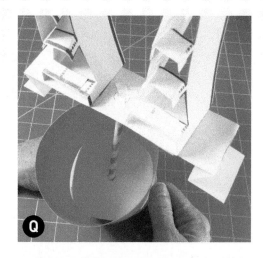

**20.** Insert the bottom of the straw into the tube and out through the hole in the bottom. Tape the ends of the strip to the tube, with one end over the seam in the tube. The springy base will curve up and leave a little space between the strip and the top of the tube.

**21.** To test the claw, hold it by the wrist and pull the straw down. The fin grippers should close (Figure **R**). Try putting a small object (nothing heavy!) in the claw to see how the grippers shape themselves to whatever they're holding!

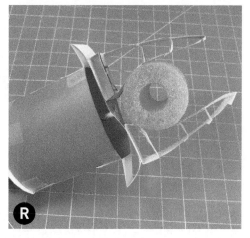

## GO BEYOND

- Can you build a claw with more fingers? (Hint: Four fingers is easier than three.)
- Try to design a flexible arm for your claw like the Festo "elephant trunk." For inspiration, check out Festo's website for students and educators. bionics4education.com.

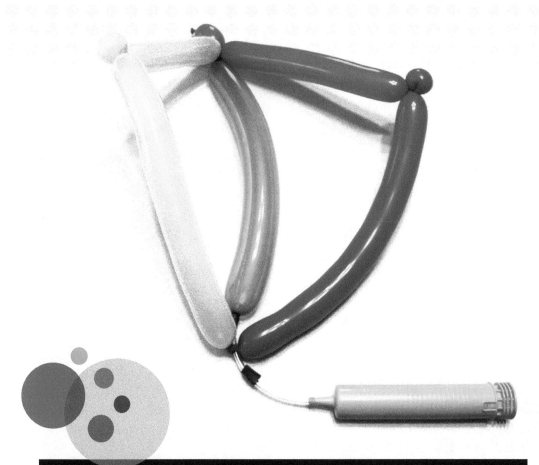

# Project: Make an Inflatable Robot "Elbow"

## FIND OUT HOW ROBOT MUSCLES BEND AND STRAIGHTEN WITH THE POWER OF AIR

Considering they started as blow-up beach toys, inflatable robots are a lot more useful than you might think! Inflatable robots (and robotic parts) are cheap, lightweight, and collapsible. They're easy to store and carry around. Plus, inflatable muscles let robots move in a more natural way than gears and motors. No wonder Disney's animated hit *Big Hero 6* featured a friendly inflatable robot named Baymax, a giant blow-up home health aide that fit inside a suitcase when not busy working.

Real inflatable robots come with different types of "skin." Small and squishy robot grippers and crawlers are made of rubber-y, stretchy material. Larger inflatable robots are often made of stiff material, like a bounce house-style trampoline. Inside, all inflatable robots have one or more chambers that can be filled with air or fluid. To make the robot bend or change shape, pumps move the air around to fill or empty different chambers.

Inflatable robots can be surprisingly strong. The huge walking inflatable Pneubotics created by Saul Griffith's research and design center Otherlab in California in 2011 looked like very odd horses or elephants and were big enough for several adults to ride on at the same time.

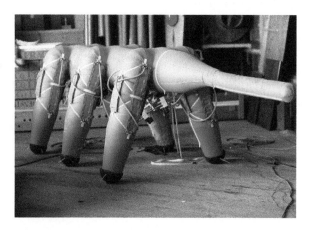

The inflatable robot "elbow" you will be building here was inspired by a type of **exoskeleton** device called an air muscle. An exoskeleton is like a robot that you wear. It helps you move more easily and can even give you super strength. In the 1950s, a nuclear physicist named Joseph Laws McKibben invented air muscles to help people like his daughter, who lost some of her ability to move when she caught a virus called polio.

Most air muscles use rubber tubing. The version you'll build is based on a project created by an engineering student named Wyatt Felt. He built a prototype using ordinary twisty balloons — the kind used to make balloon animals. (Felt went on to earn a Ph.D., partner with Pneubotics on another inflatable project, and win several soft robotics awards.) While Felt's model used a programmable air pump to fill and empty the balloons, you'll use a regular hand pump and create a valve to let the air out.

## WHAT TO EXPECT

- **Time Needed:** 1 hour
- **Cost:** Less than $10
- **Difficulty:** Easy
- **Safety Issues:** Watch out for popping balloons!

## SKILLS USED

- Blowing up balloons
- Balloon twisting techniques

## SUPPLIES

This build doesn't require anything fancy. Just make sure you have extra balloons on hand — they tend to pop!

- 3 twisting balloons and a balloon hand pump (available in party goods stores)
- Flexible vinyl tubing, 1/4 inches (15 cm) inside diameter (available in hardware stores)
- Electrical tape
- Scissors

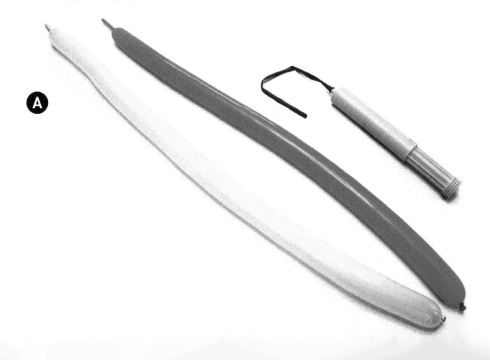

**A**

## INSTRUCTIONS

1. Take a balloon and stretch it lengthwise a few times to make it easier to inflate. Then blow it up almost all the way with the pump. Leave about 4 to 5 inches uninflated at the tip (the end of the balloon). When you take the pump off, let out a little air. This is called "burping" the balloon, and makes it easier to twist it. Tie a knot in the neck to seal it. Repeat with the second balloon (Figure Ⓐ).

2. Take one of the balloons and pinch it gently about 3 inches (8 cm) from the knot. Twist it around three times. Do the same to the other balloon, then connect the two balloons by twisting them together where they are already twisted (Figure Ⓑ).

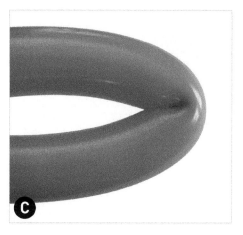

3. To make the elbow, bend one of the balloons in half (Figure Ⓒ). At the bend, pinch a golf-ball-sized section in your fingers. Twist it around three times, spinning it like a dial. Then circle it around the balloon itself until it reaches its starting point (Figure Ⓓ). Do the same with the second balloon.

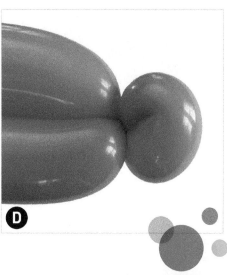

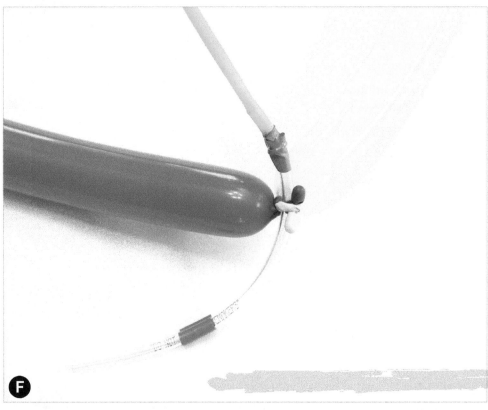

4.  Tie the tips of the balloons together using the uninflated extra rubber. Tie another knot about half an inch (1 cm) above the first. The balloons will form a diamond shape with hinges in the middle.

5.  Now take the vinyl tubing and cut a piece 10 inches (25 cm) long. To make a release valve, take the scissors and cut a small slit about halfway down. Don't let it go more than part way around. When you bend the tubing back, the slit will open to let air out. To make a seal you can open and close, cover the slit with a short piece of electrical tape (Figure **E**). If you fold over a tiny bit of the tape at one end and let it stick to itself, it makes a kind of tab that's easier to lift when you want to let the air out. Test the seal by inserting the air pump into the tubing and making sure no air comes through when it is closed.

6.  Poke one end of the tubing through the gap between the two knots in Step 4. Take a third balloon, inflate it, then let the air out. This is your air muscle. Pull the opening of the air muscle balloon over the end of the tubing that pokes out between the knots. The balloon should cover about 1 inch of the tubing. Secure the balloon to the tubing with a piece of electrical tape (Figure **F**).

7.  Take the top and the bottom of the balloon diamond and press them together. This is the movement your inflatable hinge will make. Decide how close you would like them to get, and tie the tip of the air muscle balloon to the tips of the other two balloons to hold them in this position.

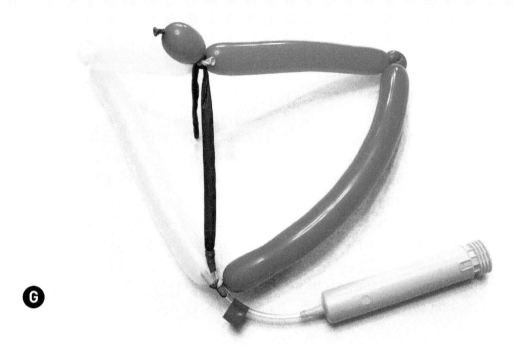

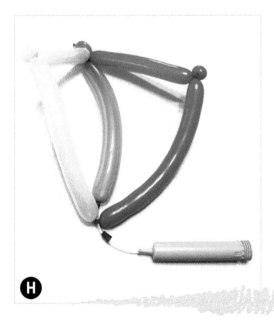

8. Insert the end of the air pump into the other end of the clear tubing, as far as it will go. Secure it with more electrical tape if needed (Figure **G**).

9. To test your design, use the pump to slowly and carefully inflate the muscle balloon (Figure **H**). As it fills with air, it should lengthen and push the balloon hinge open. To let the hinge close up again, open the release valve by unwinding the tape enough to expose the slit, and bending the tubing back to widen the opening. The air should escape and the balloon should return to roughly the same length as when it started.

## TROUBLESHOOTING TIPS

- If you're having trouble inflating the balloon, check it for leaks.
- To see if there's a problem with your pump, test it out on another balloon fresh out of the package. Watch out for cheap pumps that break easily.

## GO BEYOND

- Balloon twisting can be used for art and engineering! Learn some balloon design tips with these online lessons from Airigami: airigami.com/online-lessons.
- Invent your own inflatable robots using designs from math instead of nature. For example, in 2020 Stanford University researchers demonstrated inflatable tubes that could be bent using motorized corners that slid along their surface. Connecting several tubes into a pyramid created shapes that rolled along under their own power as the lengths of their sides were changed. Find out more at news.stanford.edu/2020/03/18/squishy-shape-changing-bot-roams-untethered.
- Custom-design an edible inflatable robot — see the instructions in my book *BOTS!* nomadpress.net/nomadpress-books/bots-robotics-engineering/.

# #2

# ROBOTS THAT GET AROUND

Explore robots that **move** in unusual ways

One of the biggest robot design challenges is making them move from place to place. Lots of robots are designed to walk, run, or jump the same way people and animals do. The Walking Robot Dog in Chapter 1 had four legs like a real dog — but robots with two, six, or even more legs are common. Other robots look like vehicles and drive around using wheels like cars or treads like tanks. Flying robotic drones are also popular. But robots can use all kinds of weird ways to travel.

Maybe you've seen ball-shaped robots like BB-8, the helpful droid that rolls around the *Star Wars* universe. In real life, an educational company called Sphero makes rolling robots about the size of a billiard ball. You can tell them where to go just like an RC car, using your smartphone as a remote control.

Then there are robots that combine the best part of legs and wheels, with legs that spin around like wheels. They're known as **whegs** (the name is a registered trademark of Case Western Reserve University in Cleveland), and look like the spokes on a wagon wheel, without the rim. Whegs can climb up stairs or step over bumpy terrain. On smooth ground, they can simply roll along like regular wheels.

Other robots just shimmy and shake where they want to go. Instead of legs swinging back and forth or wheels spinning, they use vibration motors to get from place to place. If you've ever made a brush bot by adding a tiny disk vibration motor to the head of a toothbrush, or played around with a Hexbug Nano toy robot, you know those things can move fast. These are examples of a programmable body because, by pointing the brush bristle "legs" one way or another, you can make them head in a specific direction.

Sphero

*Sphero, a robotic ball that can be programmed to jump or roll with a smartphone app, was the pioneer of rolling robots.*

Robots can also use their wiggly bodies to move. **Tensegrity** robots don't have a skeleton or any framework that holds everything together. Instead, they consist of supports (called **struts**) that never touch. The struts are connected to each other by tightly strung cords. This makes a tensegrity really springy — when you squish one flat, it pops right back into shape. Roboticist Vytas SunSpiral and others designed a tensegrity lander for NASA called the Super Ball Bot. The idea was to create a space vehicle that could bounce and tumble along the surface of other worlds, such as Saturn's moon Titan.

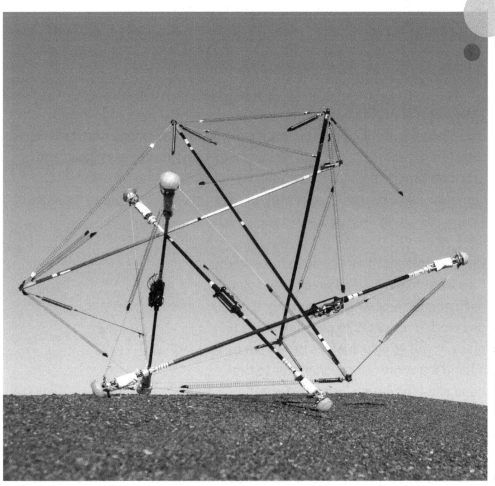

Photo courtesy of ©NASA Ames/Eric James

*A prototype of NASA's Super Ball Bot built by Ken Caluwaerts when he was a student at Ghent University.*

Paper robots based on origami, the traditional Japanese art of paper folding, can use the ability of stiff paper to unfold itself as a way to make the design move. A paper artist and engineer named Jie Qi created origami designs with programmable circuits and shape-changing wire to make them move. Today she runs a company called Chibitronics, which manufactures Circuit Stickers and other paper circuit supplies that teach students about electricity and programming.

*This paper crane flaps its wings when electric current flows through them.*

In this chapter, you'll try out robot designs that use different styles of locomotion. See what you can do with an origami frog that flashes its eyes when it hops and a vibrating tensegrity made from drinking straws and rubber bands. You'll also get to use computer software to design your own whegs. If you want, you can turn your online drawing into patterns you can cut out of cardboard, or download them to a 3D printer to produce plastic models.

# How Does an Electrical Circuit Work?

There's a lot to know about building electrical circuits, but the basic idea is this:

- **Electricity is the movement of electrons.** Electrons are one of the particles that make up atoms. (Atoms are way too tiny to see, but they are the building blocks of every kind of matter in the universe.) Electrons can hop from one atom to another. When they move, they carry energy that can be used to do work, like turning a motor.

- **Circuits are paths of *conductive* material.** A material that's conductive can carry electricity easily. That's because the atoms in conductive materials lose their electrons more easily than other kinds of materials. In most electric circuits, the conductive material is metal. But other substances, including water, the graphite in lead pencils, and your skin can also carry some electricity.

- **For electricity to flow, you need a *closed* circuit.** Before an electron will move, it needs somewhere to go. A closed circuit loops around. An open circuit has a gap, like an open drawbridge, that stops electricity from flowing. The device that opens and closes a circuit is a switch.

- **A circuit needs a power source to start electrons moving.** For the projects in this book, we'll use batteries to produce small amounts of electricity. *Electrical outlets in the wall are not safe to use in these projects!*

- **A circuit also needs a component that runs on electricity.** This can be a light, a motor, a speaker, or other components that need electricity to work. It is known as the circuit's **load**.

- **A power source like a battery has a negative terminal (end) and a positive terminal. Components have negative and positive terminals too.** For some components, it doesn't matter which end is which. But an LED will only light if the positive end is facing the positive end of the battery. This is called **polarity**.

- **To prevent a short circuit, cover the circuit with insulation, material that isn't friendly to electricity.** Insulation keeps the electricity flowing through the load. Without a load, a circuit can overheat and even catch fire. That's why short circuits are dangerous!

# Project:
# Make a Light-Up Origami Jumping Frog

## ADD AN ELECTRIC CIRCUIT TO A PAPER MODEL TO MAKE IT POP AS IT HOPS!

This light-up robot frog was invented by then-11-year-old Mina Olsson and her mom Emi, a business executive and computer engineer. To create it, they combined a traditional origami jumping frog with a light-up paper circuit project, inspired by my book *Paper Inventions*. It works kind of like a robot's pressure sensor. When you press on the frog's body, it closes an electrical circuit that turns on the frog's LED eyes. When you remove your finger, the circuit opens and the lights turn off. (See the box **"How Does an Electrical Circuit Work?"** on page 30.)

At the same time, you're creating **potential energy** that can make the frog move on its own. It's the same thing that happens when you push down on a spring — let go, and it pops back up.When you take your finger off the frog, the paper model leaps across the table. If you're lucky, it may even do a little flip!

You don't need any origami experience to make this design, but it helps to have patience. There are some tricky parts that may take a few tries to get right. Once your frog is hopping, you'll need to (temporarily) dissect it so you can insert the LEDs. Building the circuit is a snap — all you need to connect the lights to the battery is a little bit of metallic foil tape. Then fold everything back up, and your frog will be jumping and glowing in no time!

## WHAT TO EXPECT
- **Time Needed:** Less 1 hour
- **Cost:** Around $2
- **Difficulty:** Easy
- **Safety Issues:** Be careful with the coin battery. It may be a swallowing hazard for young children and pets, and can heat up if it is short-circuited.

## SKILLS USED
Folding and creasing paper into standard origami shapes

## SUPPLIES
- Copy paper, cut to 4 1/4 inches by 8 1/2 inches (or half a sheet of 8-inch square origami paper)
- 2 LEDs with medium to long wire leads (they should be the same color)
- 3V coin battery (CR2032 or similar)
- 2 small strips (1/4 inch wide) of copper foil tape with conductive glue. You can also use aluminum foil tape from the hardware store heating aisle, but you will need to fold it over so the foil side conducts electricity to all parts of the circuit.
- Clear tape (or any kind of non-conductive tape)

## INSTRUCTIONS

1.  Start by making some creases in the paper that will help you figure out later folds:
    * Bring the shorter edge at the top down to the bottom edge. Make the crease sharp.
    * Bring the same edge up to the middle fold and crease again. Open the paper up again (Figure **A**).
    * Bring one top corner down to the opposite end of the middle crease (Figure **B**). Open and repeat with the other corner to form an "X".

2.  To make the frog's head and front legs:
    * Take the X-crease on the top half of the paper (Figure **C**) and push in the sides to form a triangular "tent." Flatten the triangle (Figure **D**).
    * Fold the bottom corners of the triangle up as shown to form the legs. Flatten (Figure **E**).

3.  To make the frog's body:
    * Fold up the bottom edge to the middle crease (Figure **F**).
    * Fold in the sides so they meet in the middle. You may need to lift the front legs out of the way (Figure **G**).
    * Fold the bottom up again so it meets the bottom corner of the head. (Figure **H**)

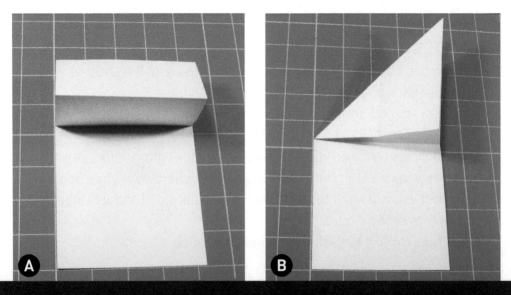

A

B

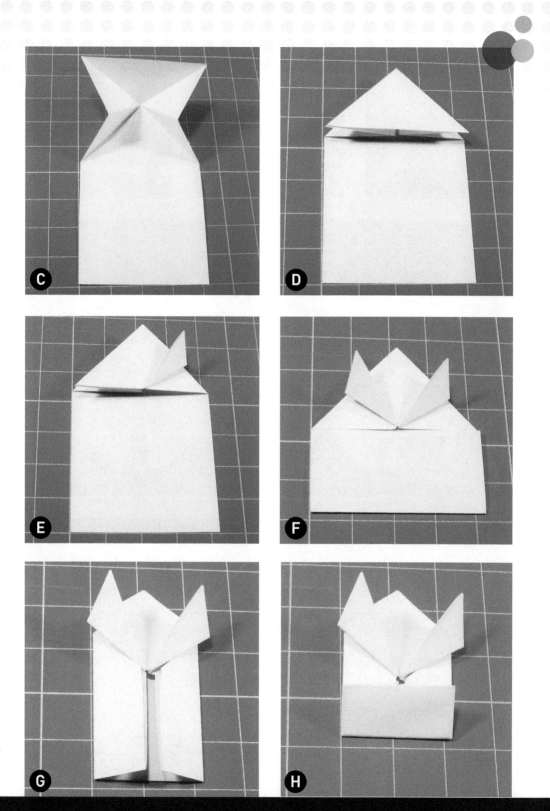

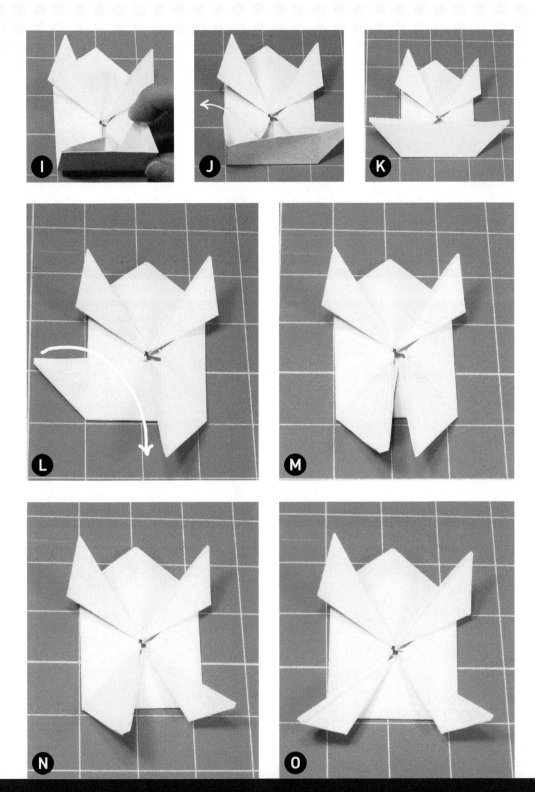

4. To make the back legs:
   - Reach inside the last fold you made in Step 3 and grab one corner (Figure **I**). Pull the corner inside-out so it forms a point sticking out the side (Figure **J**). Repeat with the other corner. The result will look like a paper boat (Figure **K**).
   - Bring the corners of the "boat" straight down so they meet at the bottom (Figure **L**), forming a diamond shape (Figure **M**).
   - Take half of the diamond and fold over the inside edge so it meets the diagonal crease (Figure **N**). Repeat with the other side to form the back legs (Figure **O**).

5. To make the springy fold:
   - Bring the bottom of the frog up along the middle crease, so the back feet are touching the front feet (Figure **P**).
   - Bring the same piece down so its bottom edge meets the middle crease. This creates a Z-shaped fold, like an accordion. Sharpen this fold (Figure **Q**).
   - Turn your frog over (Figure **R**). To test it, press down the back of the frog with one finger. Then slide your finger back to release it.

P

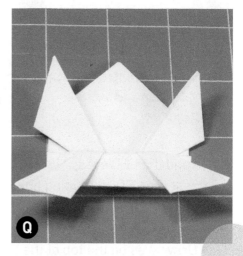

Q

R

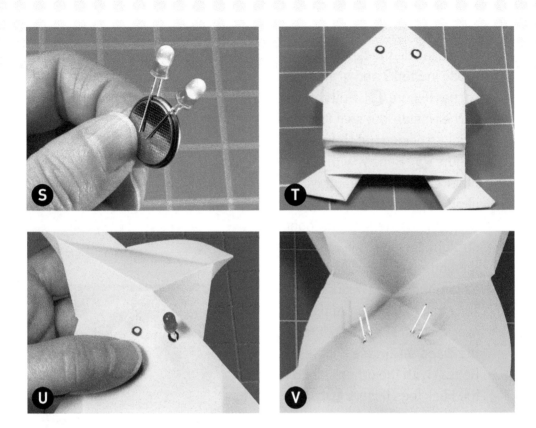

6. To add the LED eyes:
   - Test the LEDs by sliding both of them over the edge of the battery. The longer wires must touch the positive (+) side of the battery to work (Figure **S**).
   - Draw eyes on the top of the frog's head, near the nose (Figure **T**). Unfold the head. Poke the LEDs through the eyes (Figure **U**). The longer wire (the positive wire) must be closer to the nose (Figure **V**).
   - Inside the head, bend the bottom negative wires down so they're touching the paper and each other (Figure **W**). Secure them to the paper with foil tape.
   - Bend the top positive wires up and over so they cross (Figure **X**). Wrap the other piece of foil tape around them where they cross to hold them together (Figure **Y**).
   - Place the battery positive side up over the foil tape. Secure it to the paper with clear tape (Figure **Z**). Make sure to leave the upper half

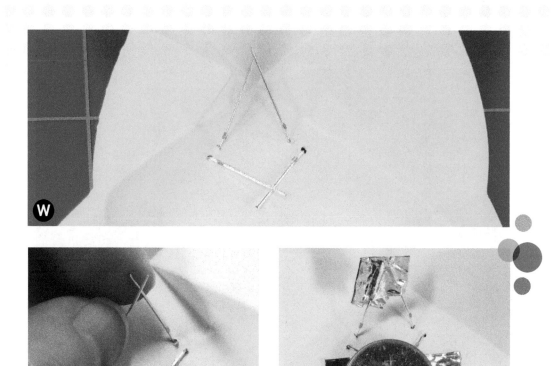

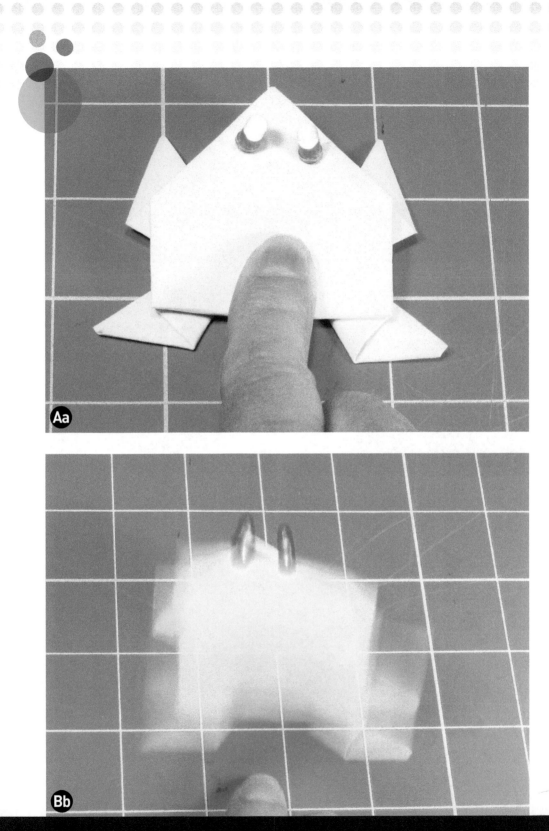

of the battery uncovered so the positive LED wires can touch the bare metal.

- Bend the positive LED wires down until they're almost touching the positive side of the battery. This is your on-off switch (or pressure sensor). The circuit closes when the positive wires touch the positive side of the battery.
- Fold the frog back up. To test your circuit, press down on the back of the frog. The eyes should light up. The positive LED wires should touch the battery to close the circuit and light up the frog's eyes (Figure **Aa**). Let go, and the lights should turn off while the frog hops in the air (Figure **Bb**)!

## TROUBLESHOOTING TIPS

If it doesn't work, look for things that can cause problems:

- **The "switch":** If the lights don't go on, try bending the top wires a little closer. If they don't go off, bend the wires a bit further away.
- **The direction of the LEDs:** Do both LEDs have their negative wires below the battery and their positive wires above?
- **The direction of the battery:** If both LEDs are facing the same way, but backwards, you can flip the battery over to make it work.
- **Loose connections:** Does metal touch metal on all connections? Is the non-conductive clear tape in the way?
- **Short circuits:** Do negative and positive wires or conductive tape touch each other, or touch the wrong side of the battery?

## GO BEYOND

What other origami designs can you add circuits to? Try the origami luna moth from Sandy Roberts' book *The Big Book of Maker Camp Projects.* You can find instructions on the Maker Camp site: makercamp.com/projects/ lightup-origami-butterfly.

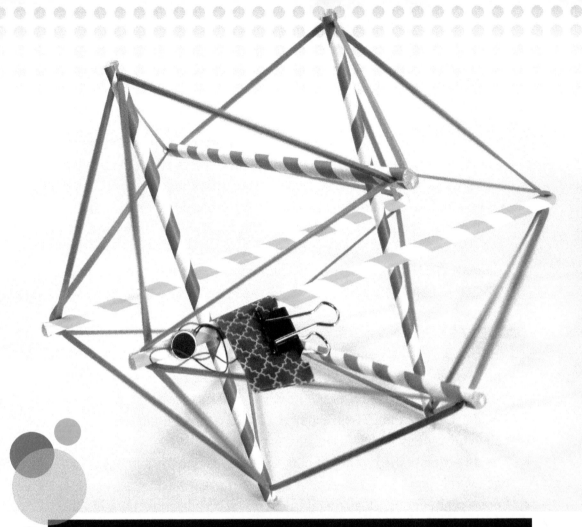

# Project: Make a Jittery Tensegrity Robot

**BUILD A ROBOT WITH ENOUGH BOUNCE TO SHAKE ITS WAY ACROSS THE TABLE.**

Tensegrities are known for being squishable and bouncy — but that's not all they do. The word "tensegrity" — a combination of the words "tension" and "integrity" — was coined by architect Buckminster Fuller, who also invented the geodesic dome. But the structures do more than just bounce. This tensegrity robot is based on prototypes developed by computer scientist John Rieffel and his students at Union College in Schenectady, New York. They "tune" their little tensegrity robots like guitar strings. Then they attach vibrating motors to make them move in different directions, depending on how fast or slow the motor is shaking.

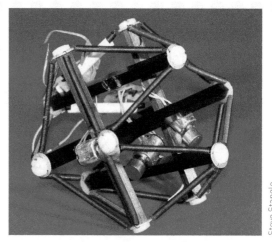

*A tensegrity robot developed at Union College which can be steered using vibration.*

Steve Stangle

To understand how tensegrity robots work, it helps to build one yourself! The directions for this drinking-straw-and-rubber-band version came from a *Make:* magazine article by Bre Pettis. It uses small rubber bands to hold the drinking straws in place while you build. When you cut the small rubber bands away, the structure pops open into its final form. Then all you have to do is add a tiny vibrating motor and a battery to make it move around. Try placing the electronics in different spots to see how the movement changes. That's the smart body at work!

## WHAT TO EXPECT
- **Time Needed:** 1 hour
- **Cost:** $5–$10
- **Difficulty:** Easy to moderate
- **Safety Issues:** None

## SKILLS USED
Making careful cuts

## SUPPLIES
- 6 rubber bands, about 7 inches long
- 6 drinking straws about the same length as the rubber bands (sturdy paper straws work well)
- 6 small thin rubber bands (such as pony tail or bracelet bands)
- Scissors

- Adhesive dots or double-sided tape
- Mini vibrating disk motor (must work with a 3V battery)
- Masking tape
- 3V coin battery (such as a CR2032)
- Conductive copper foil or nylon tape with conductive glue
- Small (3/4 inch) binder clip
- Optional:
  - Wire stripper to expose more of the motor's wire
  - Hot glue gun to reinforce the ends of the straws

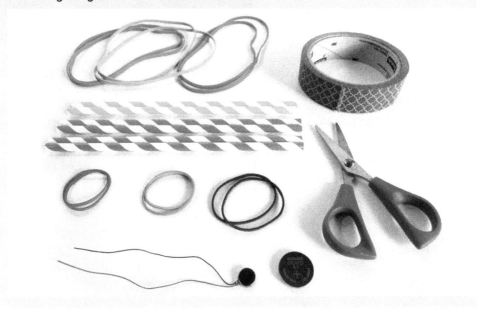

## INSTRUCTIONS

1. To make the tensegrity:
   - Cut slits on the ends of each straw. Make sure the slits line up on both ends. The slits should be around 1/4 inch deep — just enough to hold the rubber band in place (Figure **A**).
   - Line up two straws side by side. Hold them loosely in place at each end with a small rubber band (Figure **B**).
   - Do the same to a second pair of straws. Then slide the second pair between the first two straws to form an "X" (Figure **C**).

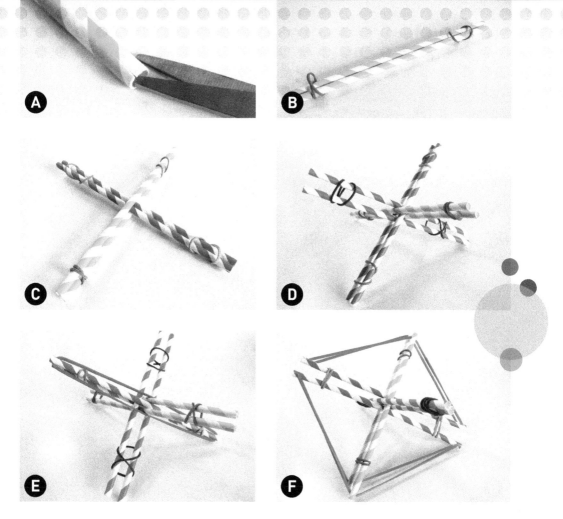

- Take the last two straws and wrap a small rubber band around one end. Slide the other end in between the second pair of straws where they cross the first pair. Wrap a small rubber band around the other end (Figure **D**).

2. To add the first big rubber bands:
    - Hold the tensegrity so the ends of one pair of straws are facing you, one on top of the other. Another pair of straws should be sticking straight up (Figure **E**). (The photos show a side view so you can see the rubber band more clearly.)
    - Line up the slits so they are both going side to side.
    - Fit a big rubber band into the slit of the upper straw facing you (Figure **F**).

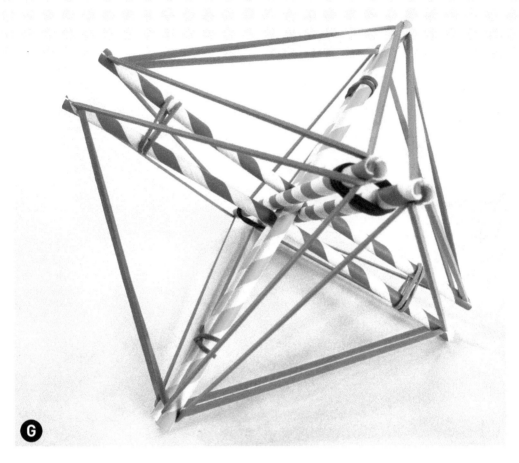

**G**

- Stretch the rubber band over the ends of the straws that are sticking up. Fit each side of the rubber band into the slits of those two straws.
- Stretch the rest of the rubber down and latch it onto the slit at the other end of the first straw. The result should look like a suspension bridge.
- Do the same with the rest of the straws. Adjust the rubber bands so they are even (Figure **G**).

3. To make the tensegrity pop open:
   - Cut away the small rubber bands (Figure **H**). Make sure none of the straws are touching. If needed, adjust the straws again so they line up with space in between (Figure **I**).

**4.** To add the circuit:

- Cut a small piece of copper tape, shorter than the width of the battery. Use it to tape one of the motor wires to one side of the coin battery. Make sure the metal at the end of the wire is touching the metal of the battery (Figure **J**).

**CAUTION:** Don't let conductive tape wrap around the edge of the battery or you could cause a short circuit!

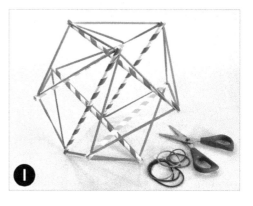

- Cut a strip of masking tape about 4 inches long. Fold over a little bit of the short ends (sticky side in). This strip of tape will be your battery holder and on/off switch (Figure **K**)!

- With the sticky side of the masking tape facing up, press the battery on one end of the tape, wire side down.

- With the masking tape still sticky side up, leave about an inch free in the middle and attach the other wire to the other end of the masking tape. Secure it with another short piece of copper tape. Again,

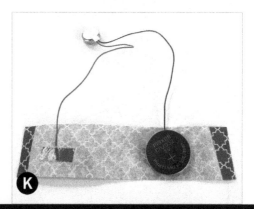

make sure the copper tape is touching the metal end of the wire.

- Use an adhesive dot to attach the motor disk to one of the straws (Figure **L**).
- Attach the middle of the masking tape to the back of the straw, sticky side facing out. Use a short piece of masking tape to hold the battery strip onto the straw.
- To turn the motor on, fold the masking tape strip up so the battery and the copper tape on the other wire are touching. Use the binder clip to hold the tape strip closed (Figure **M**).

**CAUTION:** Make sure the binder clip doesn't touch the battery! To turn the motor off, open up the masking tape strip up, with the ends hanging open away from each other.

5. (Optional) To reinforce the ends of the straws with a hot glue gun:
   - Turn the end of one straw facing up. Let a drop or two of hot glue fall into the opening until you get a rounded knob of hot glue (Figure Ⓝ).
   - Hold the straw upright for a minute until the glue cools enough to become solid.
   - Repeat with all the other straw ends.

## TROUBLESHOOTING TIPS

Things to check out if it doesn't work:
- **The "battery holder":** If the motor doesn't turn on, make sure "metal touches metal" on all parts of the circuit — the wire taped to the battery, and the other wire that gets closed up against the other side of the battery. Also make sure nothing (wire, conductive tape, binder clip) connects the two sides of the battery directly to each other.
- **The motor placement:** If the motor turns on but the tensegrity doesn't move, flip the tensegrity around so a different side is on the bottom. You can also try moving the motor closer or farther away from the end of the straw.
- **The test surface:** Find a smooth, flat surface for the tensegrity to glide around.

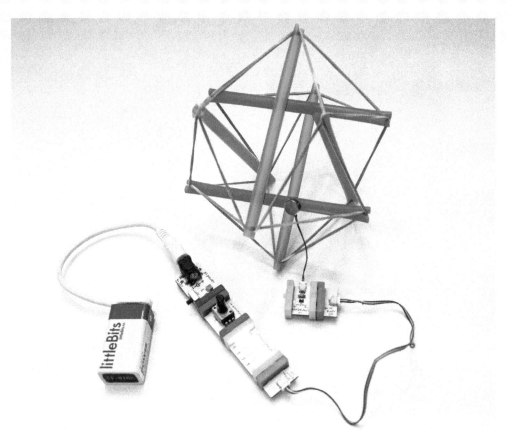

## GO BEYOND

Want to make your tensegrity steerable? Add a dimmer switch that lets you make the vibration motor go faster or slower. For instructions using littleBits electronic building blocks, check out the first edition of this book, or go to makezine.com/projects/compressible-tensegrity-robot. You can get littleBits modules and kits at sphero.com.

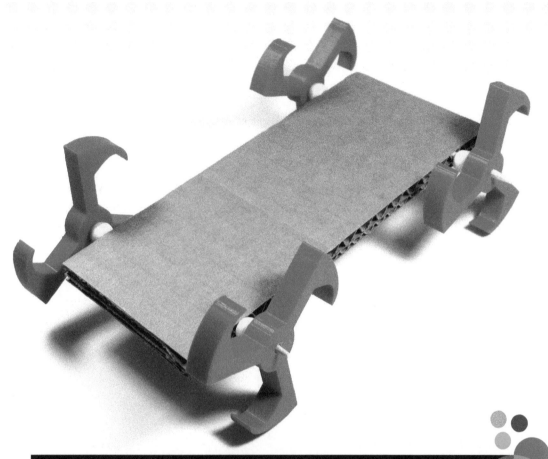

# Project: Design a Wheel-Leg Hybrid

## USE COMPUTER DESIGN SOFTWARE TO INVENT YOUR OWN VERSION OF FEET THAT ROLL!

The idea of a wheel made up of legs goes back to the ancient triskelion, a symbol with three human legs joined together in a circle. Robot whegs may have rounded feet, or even mini-wheels on the ends of their legs. Other designs just roll along on the tips of their spiky legs. In this project, you'll create your own whegs with a free design program called Tinkercad.

*Computer-Aided Design, or CAD* software is used by architects, engineers, car designers, video game designers, and more. It can be used to create

2D (two-dimensional, or flat) and 3D (three-dimensional, or boxy) drawings and animations. If you've ever created an object in Minecraft, you've used a type of CAD software.

The instructions here will help you get started with Tinkercad. You can take a pre-existing shape, such as a gear, and transform it into a wheg. Or follow the directions to make the sample three-legged version shown. This sample wheg is small, only about 2 1/2 inches across. It's flat so you can cut it out of cardboard, or 3D print it relatively quickly. The hole in the center is sized to fit on a bamboo skewer. Check out the sample design on Tinkercad at tinkercad.com/things/1RlzfX5ZoYV.

## WHAT TO EXPECT
- **Time Needed:** 1 hour
- **Cost:** Free (to create an online Tinkercad design)
- **Difficulty:** Easy to moderate

## SKILLS USED
Drag and drop graphics

## SUPPLIES
- Pen and paper
- Computer with internet access
- Tinkercad account

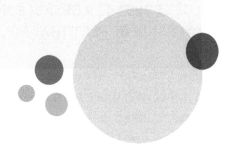

# Get Started with Tinkercad

Tinkercad is free online software that's easy to learn.
Here's what to do:

1. **Go to Tinkercad.com.** If you don't have an account, click "Join Now" and create one using an email address. If you have an account, just sign in. Any designs you create, and any shapes you "favorite," will be saved in your account.

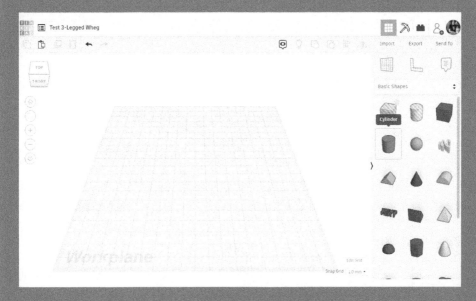

2. **On your dashboard page, click on "Create New Design."** When you start a new design or lesson, here's what you'll see:
   - The Workplane is the surface you build your object on. To see it from different angles, right click and drag your mouse, or move the little navigation box around to see the top, front, left, right, back, and bottom views. Small buttons underneath help you zoom in and out, or focus on an object you select.
   - Check out the menu of shapes along the side. If you see any you like, click on the star to add them to your Favorites list.

3. **Click on any block you like and drag it onto the Workplane.**
   Then start to build an object:
   - Click on the shape to select it and work on it:
     - To change the shape, stretch or squash it by dragging the little white boxes around it.
     - Flatten the edges or round them off by adjusting the settings in the pop-up box.
     - To lift a shape off the Workplane, drag the little black cone at the top.
     - To set it back on the Workplane, select it and type D, for Down.
     - To get rid of a shape, click on it and hit the Delete or Backspace key on your computer.
   - You can also create your own shape using the ***extrusion tool*** from the Shape Generator menu. "Mold" it by dragging around the handles in the pop-up box.
   - Add more shapes and connect them. Attach a new workplane to one side of the object.
   - When you like what you've got, select all the shapes by dragging your mouse over them. Then click on the "Group" symbol at the top to group them together. That way, they become one piece that you can move around or combine with other shapes or other groups.
   - If you want to cut an opening, use a hole (or turn a regular shape into a hole). Overlap a regular shape with a hole and group them. The hole will get cut out of the regular shape.
   - If you need to fix anything, just Undo the last step with the arrow at the top. You can also Ungroup any groups you created.

4. **When you're done, name your project so you can find it again in your Tinkercad account.** You can share the link to your project with others, or print out an image of it. You may be able to use the image as a pattern to make a cardboard prototype!

# Design Your Own Whegs in Tinkercad

To design your own wheg, first sketch out some rough ideas with paper and pencil. Look at photos of existing wheg designs for inspiration, and think about questions like these:

- What kind of surface will your whegs travel over? Do they need to be sturdy to cross hard, rocky ground? Or wide like a snowshoe for soft, sandy, or swampy terrain?
- What do you want your whegs to look like?
  - How many legs per wheel?
  - Legs bent or straight?
  - Feet flat or curved?
- How will they be attached to the robot body? If you're adding them to a toy vehicle or homemade body, make sure they fit on the axles (the rods that hold the wheels and let them spin).
- Will you try to build your whegs? If you're cutting them out from cardboard by hand, stick to simple shapes. If you're 3D printing them, make them small so they'll print quickly.

**Some ideas to start with:**

- Choose a Shape Generator gear as a base, and use the controls to turn it into a simple wheg. Add or subtract legs, make them short or long, fat or skinny, pointy or rounded.
- Follow the lesson "Make a Gear in Tinkercad" on the Tinkercad site to custom-design a gear-type wheg.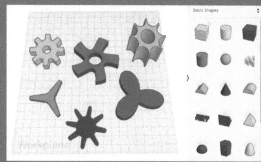
- Use the shape extrusion tool to make the legs wiggly, bend them at the knees, or add feet.

## INSTRUCTIONS

1. To make the version of a wheg shown in the example here, start with a wheel. You'll place the legs inside the wheel, to make sure the feet form a circle. To do that:
   - Drag a cylinder onto the Workplane (Figure **Ⓐ**).

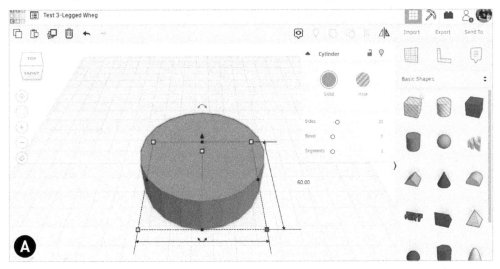

**Ⓐ**

   - Grab one of the corners and stretch the cylinder to make it 60mm wide and 60mm long. (That's about 2 1/2 inches.)

   **TIP:** To get exact measurements, click on the corner of the shape, where you see tiny white boxes. The current size will appear. Click on a white box to turn it red. Now you can type over the numbers shown.

   - Set the cylinder height to 8mm.
   - In the cylinder shape's pop-up box, click on "Solid" to change the color. A selection of colors will open. At the bottom, click the box that says "Transparent." This will let you see the legs when you combine them with the wheel (Figure **Ⓑ**).

2. To make the first leg:
   - Grab a box shape. Make it 30mm long, 8mm high, and 5mm wide.
   - Select the wheel and the leg by clicking on the Workplane and

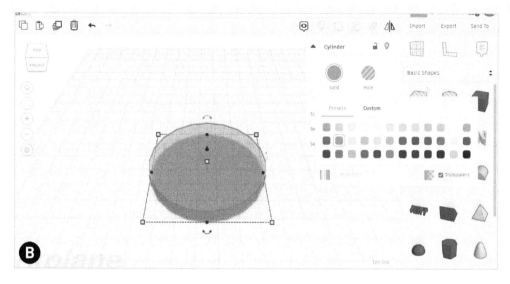

B

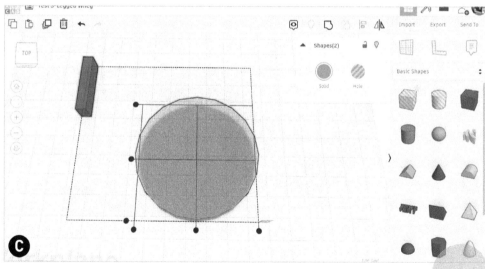

C

dragging the cursor past both (Figure **C**).
- To align the two shapes:
  - Click on the "Align" button at the top.
  - Next, click on the wheel cylinder and guides will appear.
  - Line up the leg box with the wheel cylinder by clicking the guide along the bottom of the circle.
  - Then move it halfway over by clicking the guide in the middle of the wheel.

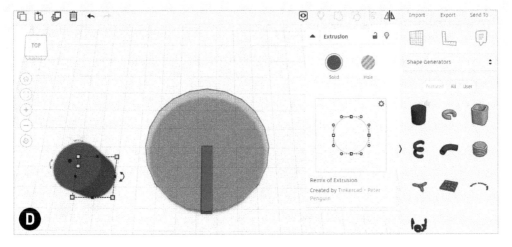

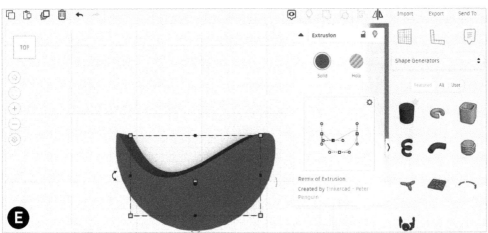

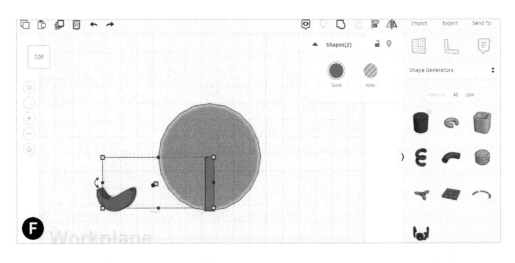

3. To attach a foot to the end of the leg:
   - Go to a top-down view using the direction control box.
   - Look for "Shape Generators" in the menu of shapes. Find the extruder cylinder shape and drag it onto the Workplane (Figure **D**).
   - Make the extrusion cylinder 8mm high. Keep the width at 20mm. The height will change as you work.
   - On the extrusion pop-up box, go to the diagram. You can change the shape by moving the little handles around. To make a rounded foot for your leg, try bringing the top handle down a little until it looks like a pointy shoe. Wiggle it around to get the shape you want (Figure **E**).
   - Select just the leg and the foot. To do this, first select everything – leg, foot, and wheel. Then de-select the wheel by holding down the shift key and clicking on the cylinder (Figure **F**).
   - Click "Align." You only want to move the foot – the leg should stay inside the cylinder. If you click the leg, the align guides should move to the box. But sometimes it's hard to select just the box, so choose either the top or bottom guides until the foot is even with the leg. You can hover your cursor over your choice before you click to see which shape will move where. Then click the guides along the bottom and back of the leg to move the foot into place (Figure **G**).

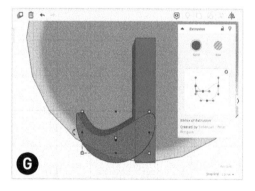

   - If you want, adjust the foot shape to fit the leg a little better by selecting it again and moving the handles in the diagram. The foot should more or less follow the curve of the wheel (Figure **H**).

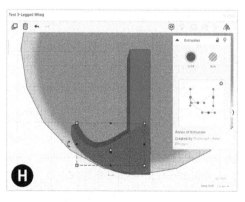

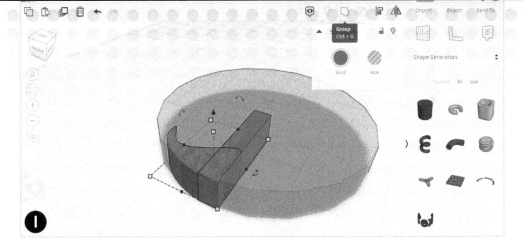

**I**

- When you're finished, select just the foot and the leg again. Click the "Group" button at the top of the screen and group the leg and foot (Figure **I**). Now you will be able to treat them as one big shape.

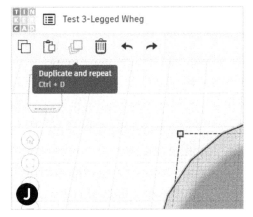

Test 3-Legged Wheg

Duplicate and repeat
Ctrl + D

**J**

4. To make the second and third legs:
   - Select the first leg and the wheel. To make the second leg, click on the "Duplicate and Repeat" button at the top of the screen, near the Tinkercad logo (Figure **J**).
   - Next, move the cursor around near the shapes until you see a little curved arrow. If you click on it, a circle with markings should appear around the wheel (Figure **K**).

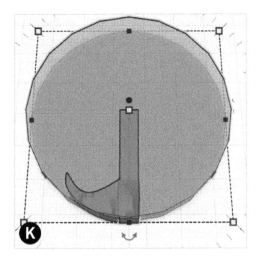

**K**

**TIP:** Make sure you've got the curved arrow for the top-down rotation guide. There are also guides to rotate the shape from the top to bottom and from side to side.

- The markings divide the circle into 360°. For a wheg with three legs, each leg will be 1/3 of the way around the circle, or 120°. Drag the curved arrow around the dial until the second leg gets to the 120-degree mark (Figure **L**).
- For the third leg, just click the "Duplicate and Repeat" button again. The third leg will automatically appear at the correct angle.

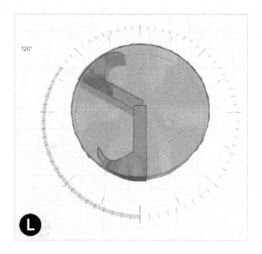

5. To make the hub of the wheg, start with the extra transparent wheel cylinders you created along with the copies of the leg:
   - First, click on the wheel and drag the extra cylinders to other parts of the Workplane (Figure **M**).
   - Make one cylinder 15mm by 15mm.

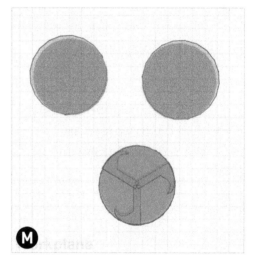

   - Give it a regular color by un-clicking "Transparent" and choosing whatever color you like.
   - Make the second cylinder 3mm by 3mm. Instead of a color, click on "Hole" to use as the center of the wheg (Figure **N**).
   - Leave both cylinders for now.

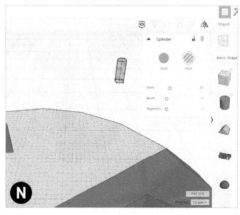

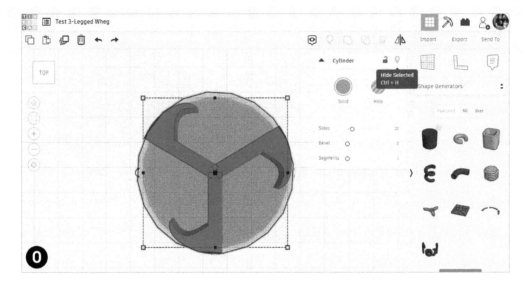

6. To connect the legs:
   - Click on the original wheel cylinder to open its pop-up window. To hide it for now, click on the little lightbulb button in the pop-up window (Figure **O**).
   - Just the three legs are left. Select them all and group them to make them into one big shape (Figure **P**).

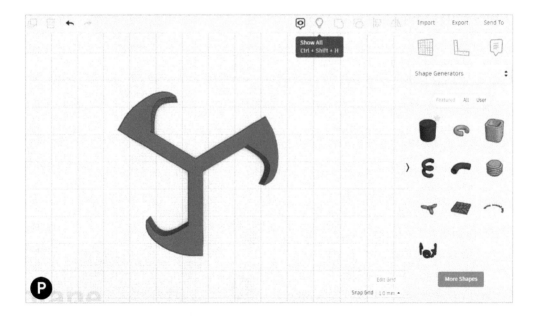

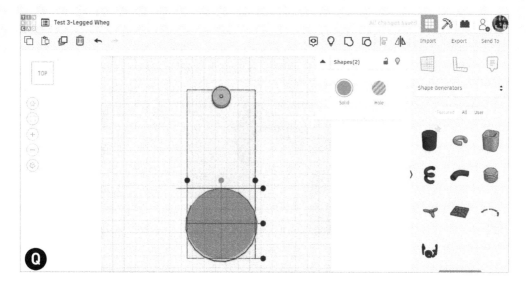

**7.** To finish the hub:
- Bring the original wheel back by clicking the lightbulb at the top of the screen.
- Select just the three-legged shape by selecting the whole wheel, then shift clicking it to de-select it. Hide the legs using the lightbulb button on the pop-up.
- Select the two hub cylinders and the wheel cylinder. Align them all to the center of the wheel, clicking on both the guide at the bottom and the guide at the side of the wheel (Figure **Q**).
- Bring the legs back by clicking the lightbulb at the top of the screen (Figure **R**).

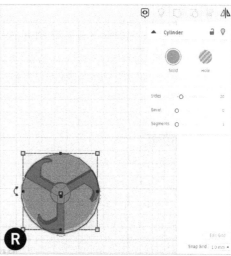

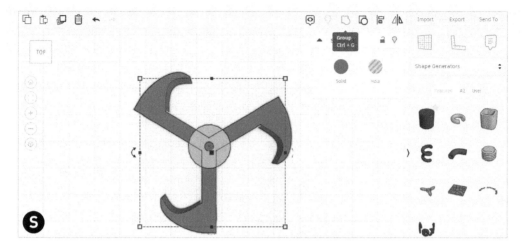

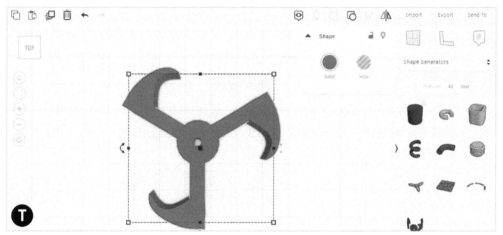

- Click on the wheel cylinder and hit the Delete key to get rid of it (Figure **S**).
- Select all the remaining shapes and group them. You're done (Figure **T**)!

## GO BEYOND

Tinkercad designs are cool on their own. But they can also be transformed into real-life plastic or cardboard models using rapid prototyping machines. Suggestions include:

- Export your design as a file to use with a 3D printer or a laser cutter.
- Switch the worktable to the orthographic (flat) view. Take a screenshot

of your project, then convert the image to a PDF that you can use with a desktop cutting machine, or print it out on cardstock and cut it out by hand.

- To test your whegs, attach them to a bare-bones platform. Make axles out of bamboo skewers — the skewers fit the hole in the wheg. They can be inserted through the "tunnels" in a piece of corrugated plastic or cardboard. Or use a pencil as an axle and insert it through an extra-wide drinking straw attachedto the test body. To test the mini wheg go-cart, let it roll down a tilted surface, pull it with a string, or add a motor.

 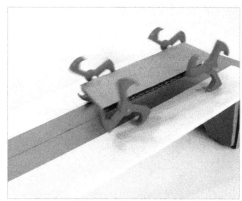

## TROUBLESHOOTING TIPS

If you've built real whegs but they don't work, take a look at:

- **The legs:** Are all the legs the same length?
- **The hub:** Is the hole for the axle or other connection in the exact middle?
- **The feet:** Are they blocking the wheg from rolling? Try making them shorter, or point the toes up a bit more. Do they slip on slick surfaces? Add some tape (sticky side out) or some rubbery craft foam to the bottom of the feet, like the soles on sneakers.

# #3

# ROBOTS THAT THINK

Use **simple coding** to program onscreen robots that talk, move, and do things on their own

All electronic robots have machine brains. But do robots think the same way animals and humans do? And does it matter?

A lot of the time, robots don't need to be that smart. If you tell them to do one specific job, that's all they need to know. Remember, the definition of a robot is a machine that can sense, think, and act. Most times, all you need to do is give a robot instructions, so it knows what to do depending on the information coming in from its sensors.

The first "programmable" robots didn't even have computerized controls. Instead, they contained electric circuits made up of sensors and transistors. When a sensor detected a certain condition, it set off a transistor that could send different signals to other parts of the robot. For instance, if a light sensor detected that it was facing a dark area, it could turn on a motor to steer the robot away from that area. When the light hitting the sensor was stronger, the sensor would send a stronger signal to the transistor, which might activate a different part of the circuit to make the robot continue forward.

Today, almost all robots with brains use computers (or mini-computers known as microcontrollers). But before a robot can think for itself, a human has to program it. To describe a condition the robot might run into and tell its computer brain what to do, they use commands like "if-then-else," "while," or "repeat until." These **conditional** commands are used in every type of computer programming.

Of course, robots don't always do jobs all by themselves. Sometimes people need to communicate with them — but machines are hard to talk to. So early computer and robotics researchers began by programming robots that only pretended to have a conversation. A robotic program designed to ask questions and give answers to humans is called a **chatbot**.

The first chatbot program, Eliza, was developed by MIT professor Joseph Weizenbaum in 1966. Eliza was designed to behave like a kind of therapist. It turned every answer from the "patient" into another question. For instance, if a user told Eliza they were feeling sad, the computer might respond, "Why do you think you are feeling sad?" Even though Eliza never said anything they didn't already know, people liked talking to the make-believe computer "therapist." Some test subjects even asked to be left alone with "her" so they could talk privately!

Today, robots use artificial intelligence, or AI, to help them sound more human. To help them learn and adapt to new situations, they tap into high-powered computers that hold and analyze information on all kinds of topics. Personal assistants like Siri and Alexa use AI to answer your questions, based on what they know about you and answers that worked for other people.

In this chapter you'll program animated robots using a free, online programming language called Scratch. Scratch was designed by the Lifelong Kindergarten group at the MIT Media Lab to help teach children the basic concepts of programming. It's drag-and-drop software, so all you need to do is find the blocks of code you need and move them around on the screen.

One of the virtual robots you'll create works on a factory assembly line. It uses its sensors and if-then-else commands to make decisions and carry out the job you tell it to do. The other is a chatbot designed to have a conversation with people. Since they're only simulations on a computer screen, you'll be able to concentrate on making them "think" without worrying about building bodies to go with them. See how useful and life-like you can make your robot characters!

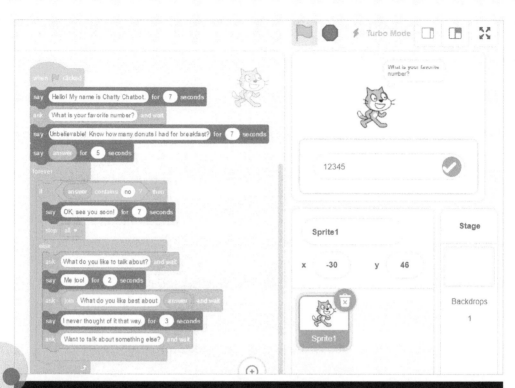

# Project: Create a Chatbot in Scratch

## CODE AN ONSCREEN CHARACTER THAT WILL KEEP PEOPLE TALKING!

Chatbots were originally designed to test how close computers were to thinking like humans. In 1950, computer pioneer Alan Turing suggested an experiment in which people had to guess whether they were talking with a computer or a human being. The "Turing Test" became the standard for judging chatbots.

What scientists have found is that to really work, chatbots need to use a little human psychology. Eliza's open-ended responses encouraged her "patients" to pour out their thoughts and feelings. On the flip side, chatbots can also keep you talking by being rude. In 1989, a student named Mark Humphrys at University College in Ireland created a chatbot with a nasty personality called MGonz. To test it, he let it answer his messages when he wasn't at his desk. One morning, he found that MGonz had traded insults with a student in the U.S. for over an hour. The American student never realized he was talking to a computer — which might make MGonz the first chatbot ever to pass the Turing Test!

In 1990, inventor Hugh Loebner created the Loebner Prize for chatbots. Programmers competed to see which of their chatbots came closest to passing the Turing Test. Each year, the best entry got a bronze medal. But no chatbot has ever won the top prize — $100,000 and a gold medal. One fan favorite is an online text chatbot named Mitsuku. It won the Loebner Prize five times between 2013 and 2019, as well as other comedy chatbot prizes. Mitsuku was created by a British musician, Steve Worswick, to entertain visitors to his site. Now owned by the company Pandorabots and known by the nickname Kuki, the chatbot makes jokes, listens to problems, and shares encouraging words. Every week, Kuki has millions of conversations with people around the world.

Modern day chatbots with AI are smart enough to understand you when you speak. But originally, chatbots like Eliza could only read what you typed. To respond, they would print out their answer or display it as text on a screen. Your Scratch chatbot conversation will be written out on the animation screen. The chatbot's words will appear in a comic-style speech bubble next to them. The person talking to them will type in their responses in a box that appears at the bottom of the animation screen. Check the Go Further ideas at the end of the project for ways to make your chatbot speak out loud!

# Scratch Basics

When you write your Scratch program — or *script* as it's called in Scratch — you will actually be creating a little interactive animation, starring characters or objects called sprites. A sprite does whatever you tell it to do — move, dance, talk (using text balloons), or make sounds (using audio files). Each sprite can have its own set of code. Each *backdrop* — the animation's background — can have its own code, too! And they can send messages back and forth to tell each other when to carry out some action. Here's how to get started coding in Scratch:

- **Sign up for a free Scratch account.** Create a username and password so you can save your projects and share them with others. (The community is safe for kids.) You will need an email address. You can also download Scratch 3 to your computer and use it offline.

- **If you're new to Scratch, run through the tutorials to help you get started.** You can also check out other people's projects. Click on "See Inside" and take a look at the program. If you want to make your own version of someone else's project, just click "Remix."

- **See what's inside the editing page.** The Scratch 3 editing page has three main sections, along with other important areas:
  - The Block Palette is on the left. It shows the different colors and categories of blocks to choose from. (The colors may differ from what is shown here.)
  - The Code Area is the center workspace for putting blocks of code together.
  - The Stage is in the upper right. It's the animation screen where your program will play.

- Below the Stage is the Sprite Pane. This area lets you change the size, position, and name of your sprite. Next to it is the Backdrop Pane.
- The Ribbon Bar along the top has links for working with your project and your account.
- Near the top, next to the tabs for Code, are tabs for Costumes and Backdrops.
  - *Costume* is the word Scratch uses for different looks a sprite can "wear." If you switch them quickly, they can be used like the frames of an animated drawing.
  - When you open the Costumes area, you will see the Paint Editor. It lets you draw your own sprites or modify existing sprites from the library.
  - If you click on a backdrop, the Costumes tab will switch to the Backdrops tab. It also has a Paint Editor you can use to create or modify your background art.
- The Sounds tab opens a Sounds Editor area. Use it to modify sounds from the built-in library or record your own. You can make them faster or slower, cut and paste parts of them, and even add a robot filter to a voice!
- Along the bottom of the screen is the Backpack. If you are signed into your Scratch account, you can pull up the Backpack space and drag in or copy pieces of code you want to use again in other programs.

- **Start to write your program by stacking blocks.**
  - Go to the Block Palette and click on any category to open up the menu of blocks it contains.
  - Drag the block you want to the Code Area workspace in the middle. Add more blocks below the first — they snap together.
  - To test how your program works as you go along, click on the blocks. Watch what the animated sprite does on the Stage (upper right of your screen).

- To move a stack of connected blocks, grab the top block.
- To copy a block or stack of blocks, right click on the top block, then click "Duplicate."
- To disconnect blocks, grab the block (or top of the stack of blocks) you want to move and pull them down.
- To delete blocks, drag them over to the Block Palette on the left and let go. The blocks will disappear.
- If a block has an oval-shaped white space, you can type words or numbers right in.
- You can also layer certain blocks on top of one another. For instance, pointy-ended blocks will snap right into pointy-ended openings in other blocks. Oval-shaped blocks will snap into oval-shaped openings.
- To repeat a set of commands, put them inside a "Repeat," "Forever," or other loop block from the Control menu (orange). The "mouth" of the loop block will stretch around the stack of blocks you place inside.

## WHAT TO EXPECT
- **Time Needed:** 1–2 hours
- **Cost:** None
- **Difficulty:** Easy to moderate
- **Safety Issues:** None

## SKILLS USED
- How to write a program in Scratch
- How to use variables to store user input
- How to use conditional commands to make decisions

## SUPPLIES
- Computer
- Internet access or offline version of Scratch 3

# INSTRUCTIONS

**NOTE:** To see the sample chatbot program shown here on the Scratch website (where you can look at the code and remix it), go to my Scratch account, RobotLady1000, and find the project called Chatty Chatbot If-Then-Else project: scratch.mit.edu/projects/624717273.

1. Before you start to program, it's helpful to plan what you want your chatbot to say and do. Think about how to make a chatbot that people will want to talk to. Here are some things to include:
   - What kind of personality you want your chatbot to have: jokester, helpful, grumpy, perky, mysterious, confused.
   - Your chatbot's task, such as playing 20 Questions, or helping you find something you lost.
   - A list of sentences your chatbot will use.

Remember, the program doesn't have to understand what the person says. It just has to give answers that make sense, even if they're random. This will help it sound "human," like the therapist program Eliza.

2. Write out an **algorithm.** An algorithm is a list of steps you want your chatbot to follow, in everyday language. When it's time to start putting code blocks together, the algorithm will help you keep track of what the chatbot should do next. An example of a basic chatbot program might be:
   - Introduce itself.
   - Ask a question.
   - Wait for the person to answer.
   - Respond using the person's answer.
   - Repeat until the person asks to stop.
   - Say goodbye.

3. Now open Scratch and create a new project (Figure **A**). If you are signed into your account, give your project a name so you can find it again easily.

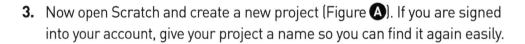

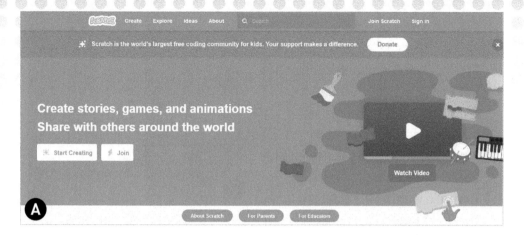

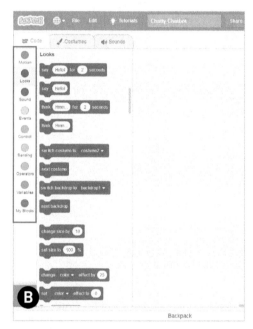

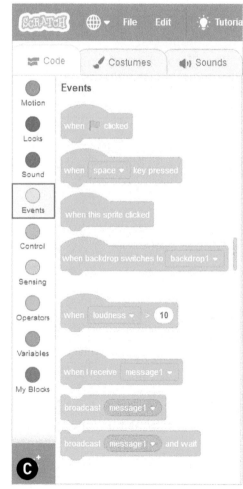

4. When the project page opens, you'll see the different kinds of code blocks and their colors on the left (Figure **B**). To start, click on Events (yellow), and drag and drop the "when [flag] clicked" block into the Code Area workspace in the middle (Figure **C**). This lets users make the program run.

5. For this project, use the Scratch Cat sprite that comes with the program. You can modify or replace it later. (You'll learn more about creating sprites and backdrops in the next project.) To make your sprite talk:

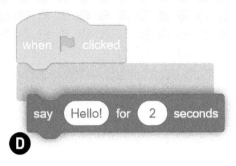

- Go to Looks (purple), and drag the "say [Hello!] for [2] seconds" block into the workspace, below the first block. It should snap into place (Figure **D**). Click on the stack of blocks and watch what happens!
- Type whatever you want your sprite to say right in the white oval (Figure **E**).
- To make it easier for people to read, add a new "say Hello" block for each line. Change the number of seconds if you want to give people more time to read the speech bubble (Figure **F**).

6. Now get the person talking:
- Go to Sensing (light blue) and drag an "ask [What's your name?] and wait" block to the bottom of your stack (Figure **G**).
- Also drag the oval "answer" block, below the "ask" block, onto the workspace, but don't attach it to anything yet. Right click (or double-click) on the "answer" oval, then click "Duplicate." You will need a bunch of "answer" blocks, so copy the original to save time.

**7.** Let the person know you heard their answer by saying it back to them. Here's one way to set it up:

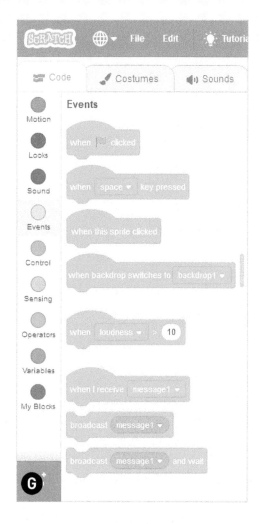

- Add a "say Hello" block and change it to respond to their answer. Keep it general, so it applies to anything they say! For example, imagine you asked "What is your favorite number?" and they answered "99". The sprite could say something silly, like, "Unbelievable! Know how many donuts I had for breakfast?"
- Add another "say Hello" block, and drag the "answer" block over the white space (Figure **H**). It will snap into place. The sprite will now say the answer given – 99!

**NOTE:** Every time a new "ask" block is used, the answer automatically changes to the newest response.

**8.** Want more of a challenge? Keep the conversation going until the person tells the chatbot they're done. You'll use an "if-then-else" block that

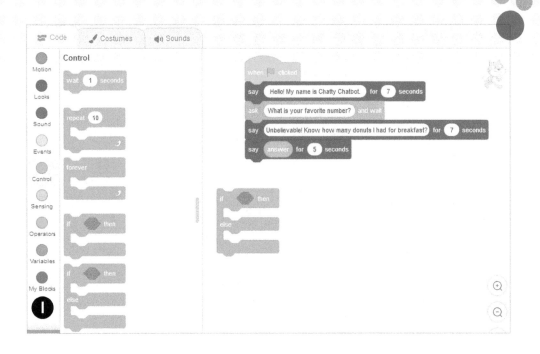

watches for the person to answer "No" when the chatbot asks if they want to chat some more. Here's how:

- Go to Control (orange) and drag an "if-then-else" block into the workspace (Figure ❶). Don't attach it to the main stack yet.
- Go to Operators (green) to get a comparison block. These blocks have pointy ends, and fit into the pointy-ended space in the "if-then-else" block. You want a block that will check for the answer "No," so you could pick a "[ ] = [50]" block. But if you also want it to work with other answers that are similar, like "Nope" and "Not now, thank you," a better choice is the "[apple] contains [a] ?" block. Find it and drag it near the "if-then-else" block (Figure ❿).

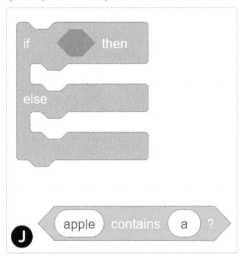

- Make another copy of the "answer" oval and snap it into the first oval space on the "contains" block. In the second space, type the word "no" over the letter "a." Then drag the comparison block over the pointy-ended space on the "if-then-else" block and snap it in (Figure **K**).

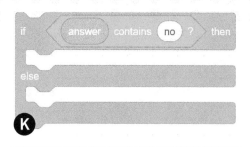

- The "if-then-else" block has two "mouths." Drag a "say Hello" block into the top mouth. Change the saying to a goodbye message (Figure **L**).

- Go back to the Control (orange) blocks and find the "stop [all]" block. Snap it in the top mouth, right under the goodbye message block. The mouth will automatically stretch to fit (Figure **M**)!

- Now build a separate stack of code that will run if the person says anything that doesn't contain the letters "no." This stack goes in the bottom mouth, under the "else." Just keep creating questions, responses, and answers as before.

9. If you want to use the person's answer in a sentence, try a "join [apple] [banana]" block from the Operators (green) menu (Figure **N**):

   - In one oval space of the "join" block, type part of the sentence.
   - In the other oval space, snap in an "answer" oval.
   - Drag the whole "join" block into a "say" or "ask" block.
   - End the "else" stack of code with an "ask" block to find out if the person is ready to leave the conversation (Figure **O**).
   - To make the "else" conversation repeat, go back to Control (orange) and drag a "forever" block into the workspace. It goes under the first part of the program.

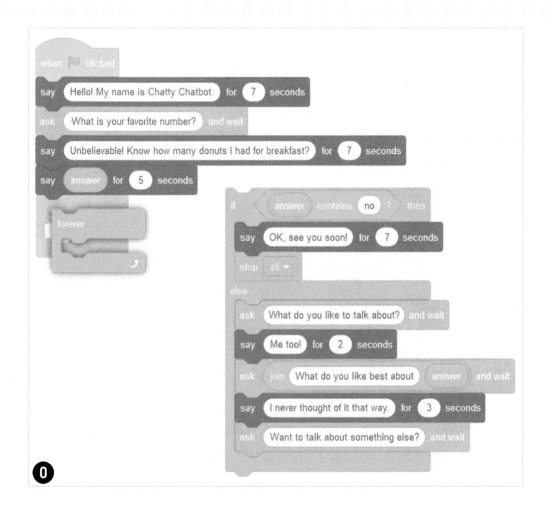

```
when 🚩 clicked
say Hello! My name is Chatty Chatbot. for 7 seconds
ask What is your favorite number? and wait
say Unbelievable! Know how many donuts I had for breakfast? for 7 seconds
say answer for 5 seconds

forever

    if  answer contains no ?  then
        say OK, see you soon! for 7 seconds
        stop all ▾
    else
        ask What do you like to talk about? and wait
        say Me too! for 2 seconds
        ask join What do you like best about answer and wait
        say I never thought of it that way. for 3 seconds
        ask Want to talk about something else? and wait
```

**0**

when ⚑ clicked
say  Hello! My name is Chatty Chatbot.  for  7  seconds
ask  What is your favorite number?  and wait
say  Unbelievable! Know how many donuts I had for breakfast?  for  7  seconds
say  answer  for  5  seconds
forever
  if  answer  contains  no  ?  then
    say  OK, see you soon!  for  7  seconds
    stop  all ▾
  else
    ask  What do you like to talk about?  and wait
    say  Me too!  for  2  seconds
    ask  join  What do you like best about  answer  and wait
    say  I never thought of it that way.  for  3  seconds
    ask  Want to talk about something else?  and wait

**P**

- Drag the "if-then-else" stack of blocks inside the "forever" block so it keeps repeating (Figure **P**).

10. You're done! Test your program by pretending to be the person using it. Answer the questions and see if the conversation makes sense. Change anything that needs fixing.

## TROUBLESHOOTING TIPS

The best way to prevent **bugs** (that's computer-speak for problems with the programming) is to try to break your own program. In fact, video game companies hire QA (quality assurance) testers to do everything wrong they can think of to see what happens. Here's how to uncover possible bugs in your chatbot program:

- Try out your program with unexpected answers. If the chatbot doesn't respond in a way that makes sense, give it more answers to watch for and more things to say. Use blocks like "and" or "join" from the Operator menu (green) to add to the possibilities.
- The best way to improve a program designed for other people to use is to get other people to test it for you! They will also give you ideas for other fun things to add.

## GO BEYOND

- Make your chatbot talk out loud!
  - If your computer has a microphone, open the Sounds tab and record yourself reading the chatbot's answers. Your spoken answers will become sound files that you can play instead of using written speech.
  - Put the person's answers in a Text-to-Speech block and hear your chatbot repeat the answers out loud. To find these blocks, click on the extension symbol at the bottom of the Block Palette column (bottom left of the screen). Choose the Text-to-Speech extension and the blocks will be added to the column.
- Make your chatbot smarter. The Scratch Wiki contains instructions for a chatbot that analyzes each word in a person's answer separately. Check it out at en.scratch-wiki.info/wiki/Creating_a_Chat_Bot.
- Try a Scratch-based AI activity to see how machines learn! The website Machine Learning for Kids has some simple exercises to test out: machinelearningforkids.co.uk.

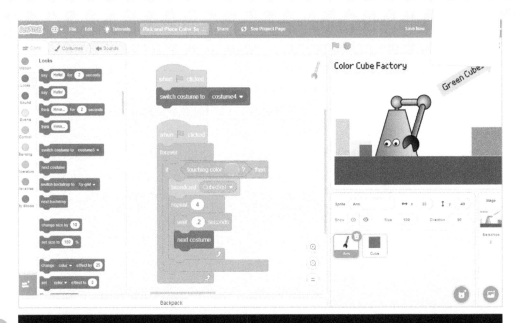

# Project: Code a Color-Sensing Pick and Place Robot in Scratch

**WRITE A PROGRAM FOR AN ANIMATED ROBOT THAT USES SENSORS – JUST LIKE A REAL ROBOT!**

One famous saying about robots is that they're good for doing jobs that are "dull, dirty, or dangerous." That's why you find a lot of robots in factories. They can lift and move heavy objects, like car frames, handle tools like super-hot plasma cutters that can be risky around humans, and do repetitive tasks like sorting items from a moving conveyor belt that are boring (and cause injuries from overuse of hands and arms).

Most **pick-and-place** robots that work on assembly lines consist of just an arm with some kind of gripper at the end, such as the fin gripper in Chapter 1. But these robots still need sensors and programming to help them figure out which items to grab, and where to put them.

In this activity, you'll use the color-sensing blocks that come with Scratch to program a virtual robot that can sort items into different areas. Follow the instructions below to make the example project: a robot arm that works on an assembly line in a color cube factory. Whenever the robot detects a green cube going by on the conveyor belt, it picks it up and tosses it into the green cube area. Once you understand how the program works, you can design your own type of sorting robot!

## Scratch Paint Editor Basics

The Paint Editor works the same for both backdrops and sprites. You can draw your own design from scratch (no pun intended), or choose a design from the Scratch library and use these same techniques to change the color, shape, or even "ungroup" and pull the separate pieces apart. You can also upload your own images and add to them.

A project can have more than one backdrop and more than one sprite. (And each sprite can have several costumes.) To duplicate a backdrop or sprite, just right click on the column on the left when Paint Editor is open. To duplicate a costume, you can also right click on it. Then you can create a different version of it.

### HERE'S HOW THE PAINT EDITOR WORKS:

1. When you open the Paint Editor, check the button below the workspace to make sure it's in Vector mode, not Bitmap. (Vector computer graphics work with shapes that are easy to resize and move around.)

2. The icons to the left of the workspace let you choose different paint tools:
   - Use the Fill box to choose a color. Move the sliders back and forth to get different tones.

- The brush and the line let you draw open or closed shapes and choose the color and shading pattern.

**TIP:** Make the line very thick to create a "rod" with rounded ends. It can be colored, just like the other shapes.

- The rectangle and the circle create closed shapes.
- The paint bucket fills in a shape with color.
- The eraser removes areas you don't want. If you need to Undo a whole step, use the curved arrows at the top of the workspace.
- The arrow tools let you select shapes to move, change, copy, or delete.
  - To stretch or squash shapes, click on the dots at the corners and sides.
  - Double click on a dot to make it disappear. (Use this trick to turn a rectangle into a triangle.)
  - The arrow tool with the dot lets you add dots anywhere along the outline of the shape.
  - Use the handle at the bottom to rotate the shape.
- If one shape is supposed to be in front of another, use the Forward, Backward, Front, and Back buttons at the top of the workspace.

3. You can Group smaller shapes so that they can be moved as one big shape. To Group shapes:
   - Hold down the shift key while you click on each shape to be added. Each will be highlighted with a blue outline.
   - Click Group at the top of the Paint Editor workspace to join them. If you need to separate them, click Ungroup.
   - To add words, click on the text tool (the big T). Click wherever you want the lettering to start in the workspace. A box will open up and let you type in letters. There are controls on top of the workspace that let you adjust the size of the letters and choose different fonts.

## WHAT TO EXPECT
- **Time Needed:** 1–2 hours
- **Cost:** None
- **Difficulty:** Easy to moderate
- **Safety Issues:** None

## SKILLS USED
- Use the Paint Editor to create a backdrop and sprites.
- Use sensing blocks like the sensors on a real robot.
- Use broadcast blocks to send a message from one sprite to another.

## SUPPLIES
- Computer
- Internet access or offline version of Scratch 3
- Tape

## INSTRUCTIONS

> **NOTE:** To see the sample program shown here on the Scratch website (where you can check out the code and remix it), go to my Scratch account, RobotLady1000, and find the project called Pick & Place Color Cube Robot: scratch.mit.edu/projects/625793764.

1. As with the first Scratch project in this chapter, it helps to jot down a quick plan of how to build your computer program. In this case, you'll need to create an animated robot, the factory it works in, and objects to be sorted by color. The algorithm might look like this:
   - Give the robot objects in different colors to analyze.
   - Tell it to look for objects that are a certain color.
   - Tell it how to sort out those objects and move them to a separate area.
   - Reset the system so it can repeat the steps with the next object.

2. Open Scratch and create a new project. If you need help getting started with Scratch, refer back to the "**Scratch Basics**" box on page 71. The "**Scratch Paint Editor Basics**" box on page 85 has tips for creating sprites and backdrops.

3. First, create a backdrop that shows the factory:

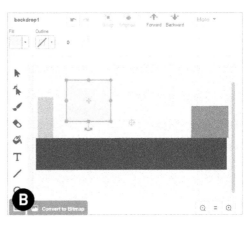

- Click on the plain white backdrop thumbnail, under the column marked Stage (bottom right). The Backdrops tab will appear at the top left of your screen, next to the Code tab. Click it to open the Paint Editor (Figure **A**).
- Use one or more rectangles or other shapes to create a factory backdrop (Figure **B**).
- Along the bottom, make a long rectangle that goes across the whole stage. This will be the conveyor belt where the robot works.

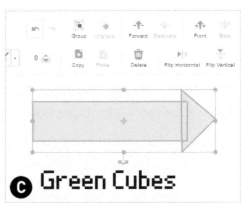

- Add a sign to show where the green cubes will go. This arrow was created by grouping a rectangle and a triangle, just like the way you joined shapes in Tinkercad in Chapter 2. To add wording, click on the big T for "text" in the menu on the left. Remember, the robot will be looking for green objects. If there's anything green in the backdrop, make sure the robot can't touch it (Figure **C**)!

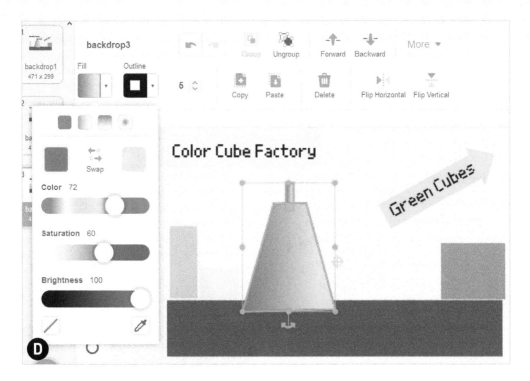

4. In this example, only the robot's arm really needs to be animated. That means you can draw the robot's body right in the background. Some details you can add:

   • To make the robot stand out, use the color controls to add an outline and shading (Figure **D**).

   • Give the robot a face to make it seem more human (Figure **E**). (See Chapter 4 to learn why people prefer robots with googly eyes!)

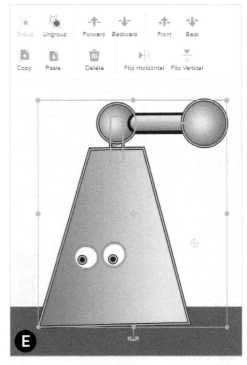

- To show that the robot is standing behind the conveyor belt, use the Backwards button to send the robot shape behind the long rectangle (Figure **F**).

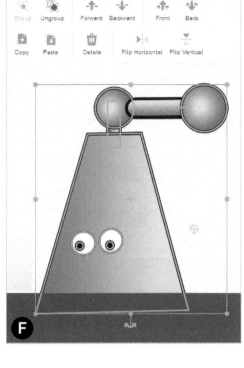

5. Next, replace the Scratch cat with a new sprite for the robot's movable arm:
   - In the Sprites Pane below the Stage, right click on Sprite1 and to delete it (Figure **G**).
   - Open the "Choose a Sprite" menu and click on the paintbrush to start building a new sprite. You can give this sprite a name — Arm — by typing over Sprite1 in the space above.
   - Go to the Costumes Paint Editor. To draw the robot's arm, use a rectangle or thick line, or draw your own shape. Remember, the arm

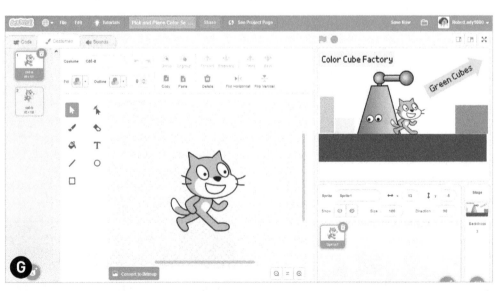

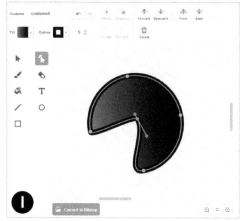

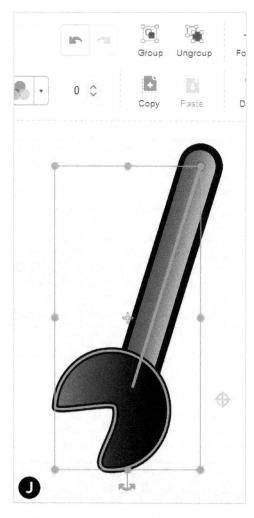

needs to be long enough to touch the cubes going by on the conveyor belt (Figure **H**).

- If you want, add a gripper to the end of the robot's arm. You can custom design the shape using the same kind of controls as in Tinkercad (Figure **I**).

- Make sure to group all the pieces of the arm together, so they act like one shape (Figure **J**).

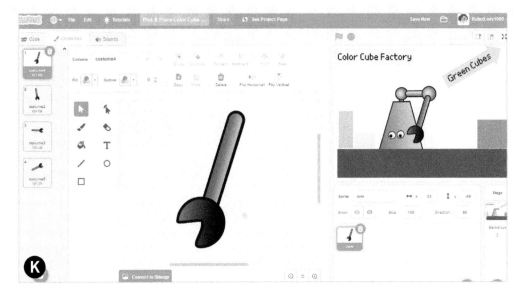

- As you create your arm sprite, keep an eye on the stage (upper right of the screen) to see how it fits in with the rest of the scene (Figure **K**). Don't worry about animating this sprite just yet — you can do that when you are coding.

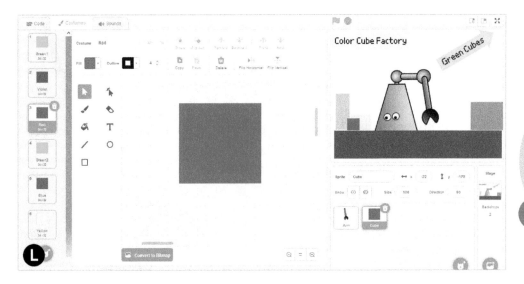

6. Now it's time to create the cubes. Since you only see one cube at a time, you can create one cube sprite and tell it to change to a different costume every time it goes by (Figure **L**). If you make the costume

changes random, it will make the animation more fun to watch. Here's what to do:

- Create a new sprite and give it a name, like Cube.
- Use the rectangle tool to make the first cube. Check the Stage to be sure it's the right size for your backdrop. Then use the Fill tool to make it whatever color you like.

**IMPORTANT:** Don't put an outline on this sprite! The color of the cube needs to touch the robot arm. If the Outline is on, click the red slash to turn it off.

- Name the costume with the color of the cube. Then right click on the first cube costume to duplicate it. Change the color of the second costume and give it a name that matches.
- Continue making as many costumes as you like. Remember to make at least one of them green! If you have a lot of different costumes, add a few more green costumes so they pop up more often.

With all your artwork done, you're ready to code! Start with the Cube sprite. The algorithm for it looks like this:

- Move one cube at a time from left to right along the conveyor belt.
- At the end of the conveyor belt, make these things happen instantly:
  - change the cube's color randomly,
  - send the cube back to the beginning of the conveyor belt,
  - start the cube moving along the conveyor belt again from left to right.
- If the robot broadcasts a message that the cube is green,  make the cube change direction and fly off toward the Green Cubes sign.

7. To use blocks from the Motion (dark blue) menu to make the Cube sprite move to the right:

- Drag a "move [10] steps" block into the workspace. Click on it to see the sprite move a short distance to the right (Figure **M**).
- Put the "move [10] steps" block inside a "forever" block from Control (orange). Click on this stack to make the cube move across the whole stage. Notice that the cube stops moving when it hits the right edge of the Stage.

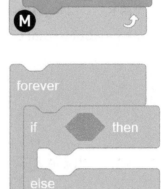

8. To make the Cube sprite go back to the beginning when it reaches the end of the conveyor belt:
   - Drag an "if-then-else" block from Control inside the "forever" block (Figure **N**).

   - Drag the "move" block inside the mouth below "else." Change the number of steps to 2. This will make it move slower.
   - Go to the Sensing menu (light blue) and drag the pointy-ended "touching [mouse-pointer]?" block inside the space on the "if-then-else" block. Click on the little arrow next to "mouse-pointer" and change it to "edge" (Figure **O**).
   - To make the Cube sprite jump back to the right spot:
     - In the Motion menu, find the "go to x: [] y: []" block — but don't grab it yet (Figure **P**).
     - Go to the Stage, drag the Cube sprite to the beginning of the conveyor belt, and drop it. Watch how the numbers on the "go to" block change! (The numbers refer to the cube's location on an invisible grid. You can find any location by looking at the x and y numbers of the square it's on. To see the grid, search for it in the Backdrops library.)

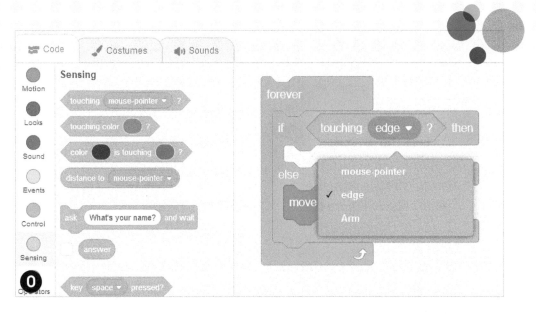

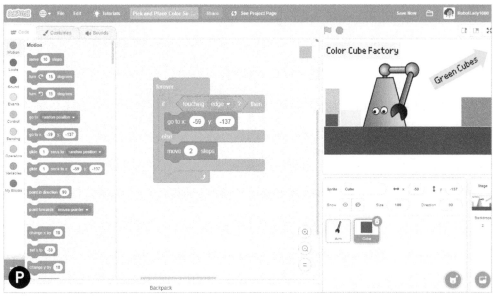

- Now drag the "go to" block into the remaining mouth of the "if-then-else" block. Try dragging the Cube sprite to a different part of the Stage. Click on the stack of code to make sure the cube goes back where you want it to, and then moves along the conveyor belt over and over.

9. Next, make the Cube sprite change costumes, so the color changes each time it comes down the conveyor belt:

- Go to the Looks menu (purple) and drag a "switch costume to [costume name]" block above the "go to" block (Figure **Q**).
- Go to the Operators menu (green). You will see blocks that look like math operations. Drag the "pick random [1] to [10]" block over the name area on the "switch costume" block.
- Count the number of costumes you have, and type that number over the 10.

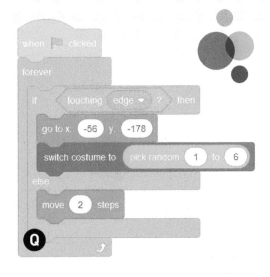

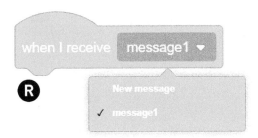

10. From the Events (tan) menu, drag a "When [flag] clicked" block on the top of the stack. Click on the stack to make sure everything is working!

11. Now create a new stack of code telling the cube to change course when it receives a message from the robot arm saying that a green cube has been detected. The cube needs to fly through the air in the direction of the Green Cubes sign. To begin:

- Go to the Events menu (tan) and look for "when I receive [message1]." Drag it into an open area in the workspace (Figure **R**).
- Click on "message1" and create a new message. Give it a name like CubeSort.
- On the Stage, move the cube to the right edge near the Green Cubes sign (Figure **S**).

- Go to the Motion menu and drag a "glide [1] sec to x: [] y:[]" block. The numbers should be the current position of the Cube sprite, at the right edge of the stage near the Green Cubes sign.

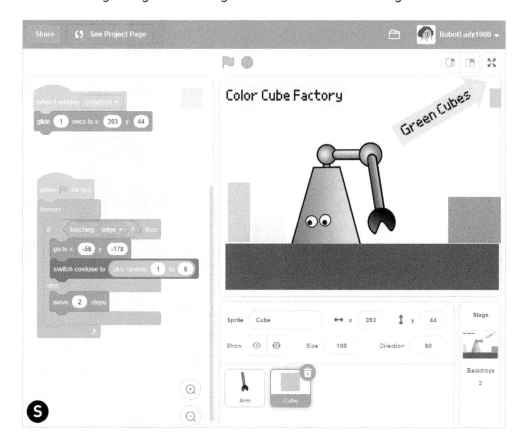

**12.** Before moving on, test out the program:
- Click the green flag to run the program.
- To save time, instead of waiting for a green cube to appear at random, open the Cube sprite's Paint Editor and click on a green costume.
- When the green cube touches the robot arm, it should glide up to the point near the Green Cubes sign.
- When it reaches the edge of the stage, it should instantly go back to the original starting position and start again.

13. To finish off the program, add a
   few costumes to the Arm sprite
   to make it look like it is tossing
   the cube in the direction of the
   Green Cubes sign (even though
   the cube is really moving by
   itself). To animate the Arm:
   - Right click on the first
     costume and duplicate it.
   - On the second costume,
     check that any separate
     parts of the arm are grouped
     together (Figure **U**).
   - Click on the arm to make the box
     with the curved handle appear.
     Grab the handle and swing it up
     a little to rotate the arm. You only
     need to move it a little from the first position.
   - Repeat two or three more times, ending with the
     arm in position to let the cube fly (Figure **V**).

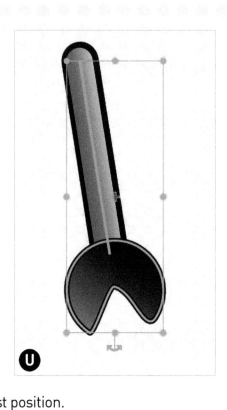

**U**

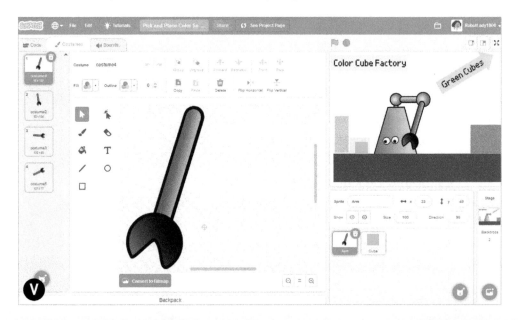

**V**

**Now let's code the Arm sprite. Its algorithm looks like this:**

- Test each cube as it goes by to see if it is green.
- If the cube is green:
  - Broadcast a message to the Cube sprite.
  - Wait for the cube to start flying away from the conveyor belt.
  - Switch costumes to show the arm moving with the cube.
- Move back to the starting position.

**14.** To make the Arm sprite broadcast a signal to the Cube sprite:

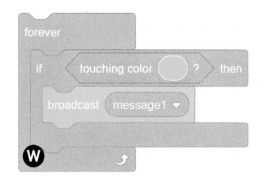

- Go to the Control menu (orange). Drag a "forever" block onto the workspace (Figure **W**).
- Drag an "if-then" block inside the "forever" block. (You don't need the "else" for this one.)
- Go to the Sensing menu (light blue) and drag a pointy-ended "touching [color]?" block into the space on the "if-then" block. Change the color to green.

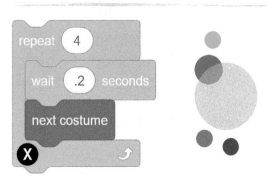

- From the Events menu, drag a "broadcast []" block inside the "if-then" block. to "CubeSort" as the message.

**15.** To animate the robot arm:

- Go to the Control menu and drag a "repeat [10]" block into the workspace. Don't connect it to other blocks yet (Figure **X**).
- Go to "Looks" and find the "next costume" block. Drag it inside the "repeat" block. Set the number of repeats to the number of costumes for your Arm sprite.

- Click on the repeat block to watch the arm move. It should end up at the starting position. If not, adjust the number of repeats. If you want to make it change positions a little slower, go to Control and find a "wait [1] second" block. To set the wait to half a second, type 0.5 over the number 1. To make it go a little faster, set it to 0.2.

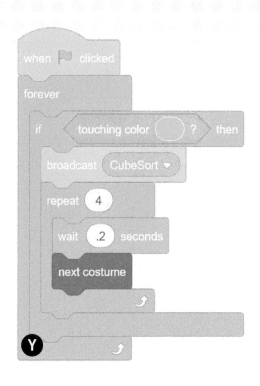

- Drag the "repeat"stack of blocks inside the if-then block, below the broadcast block (Figure **Y**).
- Top the stack with a "when [green flag] clicked" block from the Events menu.

**16.** You're done! Test out the whole program by clicking on the green flag (Figure **Z**).

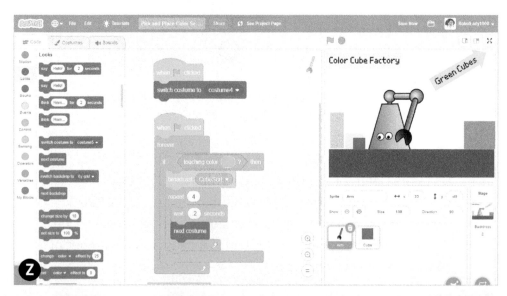

## TROUBLESHOOTING TIPS

- If the robot arm gets stuck in a weird position, add a new "when [green flag] clicked" stack with a "switch costume" block. Set it to the first costume, so you can always stop the program and reset the arm.

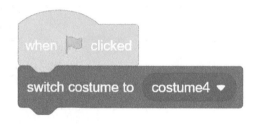

- If you don't like where the sprites are moving, you can go back and drag objects around in the backdrop, including the robot body.

## GO BEYOND

- Go to the Sound block menu (violet) and insert some sound effects from Scratch's sound library. For example, you can add a block that says "play [Low Swoosh] until done" to the Cube sprite's "broadcast message" stack of code.
- Choose a piece of music from the sound library and play it in a loop over your program.
- Give your robot factory worker a break by ending the program when it has sorted 10 green blocks. To do that, create a counter using the Variables blocks (dark orange). Every time the Arm sprite touches green, make it add 1 to the counter. When the counter reaches 10, you can end the animation with a "stop all" block from the Control block menu.

# #4

# MAKING ROBOTS LIKABLE

Find out why robots can seem **cute** — or **creepy**

Robots that look like machines — like the pick-and-place robot in Chapter 3 — are efficient, but hard to warm up to. That's why scientists in the field of **social robotics** look for ways to help people and robots get along. One way is to make robots easier to talk to, like you did with the chatbot in Chapter 3. Another is to bump up the cute factor.

For example, take two robots you may know from *Star Wars*: R2-D2 and C-3PO. Both droids are designed to be people-friendly, but in different ways. C-3PO is a gold-colored humanoid robot who can speak millions of languages and is programmed to get along with different alien species. His companion, R2-D2, is shaped like a fire hydrant, and can only beep and whistle when he has something to say. Still, people can understand R2, just like they know what it means when a dog leads you to the door ("It's time to go out!"). C-3PO is better at communicating facts and figures. But many fans think the little droid is more lovable.

Becca Henry

Making robots look, act, and talk just like humans is hard. But many robot designers keep trying — even though it's not always the best way to make robots relatable. The problem is something called the Uncanny Valley. It's a theory that says people prefer robots that either look obviously fake or totally real, but not in-between. Think about it — if you met someone and couldn't tell if they were human or a robot, would you find them interesting? Or a little creepy? (Or both?)

That's the reason many roboticists make their machines look more like cartoon creatures than real people. Professor Cynthia Breazeal — who invented the term "social robots" — founded and leads the Personal Robots group at the MIT Media Lab. She and her team have created many robot prototypes that borrow features from baby animals: big eyes, large perky ears, and soft fur. In 2002. Breazeal created the robot "Leonardo" with the Stan Winston Studio, a Hollywood special effects company. Leonardo was a furry **animatronic** (programmable doll or puppet) that looked like a cross between a puppy and a human toddler. When you talked to Leo, it would search your face with its huge eyes and show its feelings by swiveling its ears around and gesturing with its little hands.

Designers like Carla Diana, author of *My Robot Gets Me*, believes **social design** can even help robots that definitely look like machines. How do you know what your robot vacuum cleaner is trying to say when it plays a series of notes and stops moving? If the music sounds worried, it may be stuck under the couch. If it plays a happy tune, it's probably just finished cleaning the carpet. Social design doesn't have to be fancy. It can be as simple as giving the machine some googly eyes. Here are some of Diana's tips for helping any robot get along better with people:

- Make it clear where the front of the robot is. This lets people know when they are "facing" the robot so they can watch and listen for messages. It also helps them figure out what direction the robot will head in when it starts to move.

- Your robot needs the ability to send messages to people nearby, such as "Help, I'm stuck!" or "I'm running out of battery." So give your robot one or more ways to communicate. These can include:
  - Lights
  - Sounds
  - Gestures and body language, such as twisting to indicate where it's looking, or nodding up and down to show it agrees.
- Design your robot to fit in with its environment. If it's a household robot, you might want it to blend in with the decor. Just make sure it's still visible, so people don't trip over it.

In this chapter, you'll play around with making robots more friendly — or more weird. First, you'll see how you'd look as a robot, and try to make your double fall into the Uncanny Valley. Then you'll create a soft, stuffed plushie and give it a real robot brain: a mini-computer known as a ***micro:bit***! You'll program your squishy robot to roll its googly eyes and answer questions with robot noises using free, online, software called MakeCode.

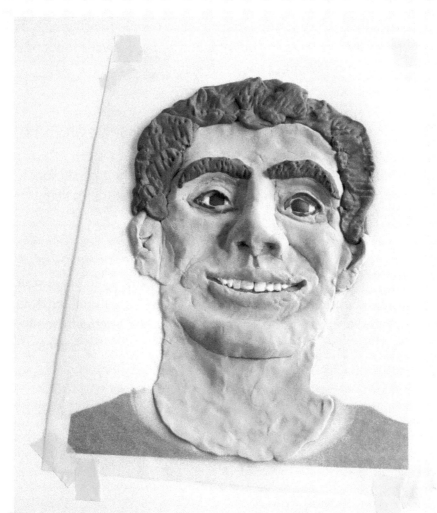

# Project: Picture Yourself in the Uncanny Valley

## CREATE A ROBOT FACE THAT LOOKS A *LITTLE* TOO MUCH LIKE YOU.

The Uncanny Valley was first described by Japanese roboticist Masahiro Mori in 1970. He noticed that people reacted differently to someone with an artificial hand if it looked more like a tool than an actual hand. So Mori did an experiment. He asked test subjects to rate how much they liked different pictures of people, from cartoons to photographs. The more real the picture, the better the test subjects liked them. When he put the test results on a chart, it looked like a line that kept going up as the images became more real. Right before the end, however, the line took a sharp dip downward and then came back up, like a valley between two mountains. Mori concluded that when the image looked *almost* human but not quite, it went from being friendly to scary.

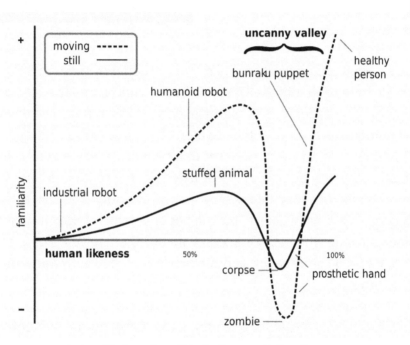

*A simplified version of Mori's Uncanny Valley diagram.*

Karl MacDorman under a GNU Free Documentation License

It took many more years before robots looked human enough to fall into the Uncanny Valley. Some of the first were created by roboticists who were also artists. David Hanson graduated from the Rhode Island School of Design. He got his start working for Disney, creating animatronic statues that moved and talked like humans. His company Hanson Robotics builds very life-like robots. Some are made to look like famous people, including scientist Albert Einstein and science fiction author Philip K. Dick (who wrote about robots that didn't realize they weren't human). Hiroshi Ishiguro, a roboticist at Osaka University in Japan, first studied to be a painter. After he became interested in computers, Ishiguro built a robotic clone of himself named Geminoid. He sent it out to give lectures in his place, making it move and talk by remote control. To make it even more lifelike, he even topped it with his own hair.

Hiroshi Ishiguro via Osaka University

*Hiroshi Ishiguro and his robot Geminoid HI-4.*

For many people, realistic robots like those created by Hansen and Ishiguro definitely fall into the Uncanny Valley. But no one is sure how the Uncanny Valley reaction works. Some experts think it may have developed in early humans as a survival tool, to alert them to anyone who might be sick. Others, including David Hanson, don't believe it exists at all. The way the robot moves may be part of it. For example, the robot dog Spot can seem frightening because it looks like a machine but walks like a real dog. Even passive-dynamic walkers like the paper version of Spot in Chapter 1 can look strange when they walk downhill by themselves! The Uncanny Valley may also be one reason zombie movies can be funny and scary at the same time.

Hiroshi Ishiguro's goal is to create a robot that looks human enough to pass the Turing Test. But Masahiro Mori believes a better solution to the Uncanny Valley problem is to make it obvious that the robot isn't real. In 2021, the British robotics company Engineered Arts tried to do that with its realistic robot, Ameca. Instead of hiding Ameca's tubes and wires, they let them stick out. The robot's rubbery skin is gray. But Ameca's facial expressions still look eerily real to many people. Even Tesla founder Elon Musk — whose electric car company is also working on its own robot, named Optimus – responded to a 2021 video of Ameca by tweeting "Yikes!"

For this project you will explore the limits of the Uncanny Valley by making a copy of your own face using modeling clay. You don't have to make an entire head — just add clay to a flat picture to sculpt the parts that stand out, like your nose, lips, and chin. Will it be cool or creepy? Take a poll of friends and family to find out!

## WHAT TO EXPECT

- **Time Needed:** 1–2 hours
- **Cost:** $15 or less
- **Difficulty:** Easy
- **Safety Issues:** None

## SKILLS USED

- Playing with modeling material.
- Making a life-like model.

## SUPPLIES

- 1 or 2 copies of a black-and-white selfie, printed out on letter-sized regular paper (see tips below for how to shoot it and how to pose)
  - If you can't print out a photo, get a mirror and draw a sketch of your face.
- Masking tape, glue stick, or spray glue
- Cardboard or poster board to use as a base
- Crayola Model Magic modeling compound, or other rubbery, self-drying material, white or colored to match your skin
- Washable markers for adding color to the modeling compound
- Clay modeling tools or kitchen utensils, including:
  - Unsharpened pencil with clean eraser
  - Toothpicks
  - Craft sticks
  - Disposable forks, knives, and spoons

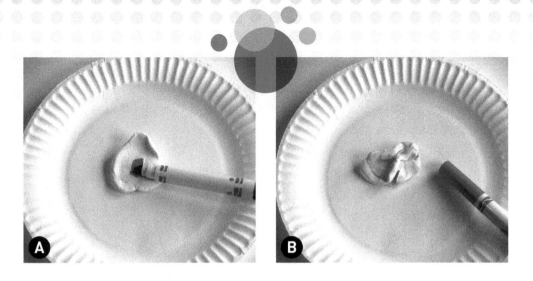

## INSTRUCTIONS

1. As you plan how your photo should look, think about ways to make your clone look believable but eerie at the same time:
    - Make your features — ears, eyes, nose, mouth — stand out from your face as much as possible.
    - Include details like individual teeth and the shape of your nostrils.
    - Give your image extra personality and emotion.
    - Add things like jewelry or hair color that make you look unique.
2. If you want to match your exact skin tones, take a hunk of Model Magic and flatten it into a thick pancake. Then roll the tip of a washable marker back and forth across the pancake's top (Figure **A**). Smush and knead the ink into the compound until the color is even (Figure **B**).
3. Tape or glue one copy of your photo to poster or cardboard (Figure **C**). Begin to sculpt your prototype with Model Magic. Use a second copy of your photo if you need a guide when you begin to cover up the first copy.
4. Start with the highest parts first: the nose (Figure **D**), chin, and brow (Figure **E**). As you build, use the smallest amount possible. It's easier to add more than to take away extra.
5. After you've built the highest parts, go on to other rounded areas like the cheeks and the area around the lips (Figure **F**).
6. Once you've got the most obvious shapes laid out, fill in the flat areas between them, like the forehead and the neck (Figure **G**). As you add each piece, connect it to what's already there.

7. Pay attention to the unique shape of your eyes, the inside of your nostrils, and the curves inside your ear. Add each individual tooth, one by one (Figure **H**). These little details are the things that make the model look hyper-realistic.

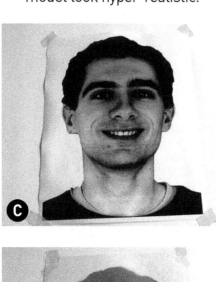

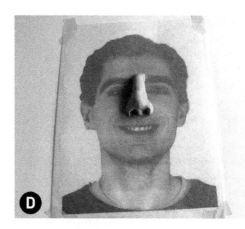

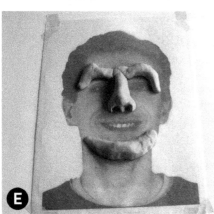

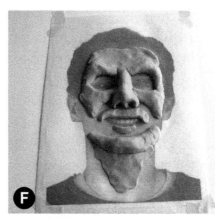

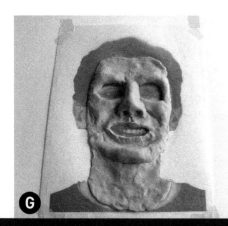

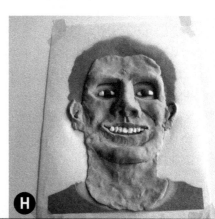

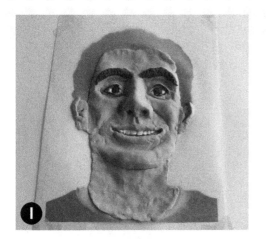

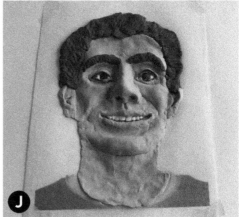

8. Fill in any sunken areas that are left, such as around the eyes. Use a disposable spoon or other carving tools to create an overhang under the eyelids and add lines and creases (Figure ❶).

9. Sculpting hair with Model Magic can be difficult. Try rolling skinny clay snakes for eyelashes and eyebrows. You can also spread a very thin layer of modeling compound for the hair and "draw" individual strands into it, using a fork or carving tool. Adding hair in clumps will give it more dimension (Figure ❶).

10. Use markers to draw pupils on the eyes and add other spots of color.

11. Leave your finished design out overnight to dry. You may need to leave it for a couple of days to dry completely.

12. To test how close you came to the Uncanny Valley, take a survey of friends and family. Ask them how your clay face makes them feel. Are they happy to see "you?" Or does it seem too weird to be real?

## TROUBLESHOOTING TIPS

As you're working, keep these things in mind:

- Be careful not to mash up a part you've already finished when you go on to another part.
- Try to keep colors from running into each other. Be especially careful not to mix the white of your eyes and your teeth with the skin and eye colors around it.

## GO BEYOND

- For even more realism, add some shine to the eyes, teeth, and lips to make them appear alive and moist. Take a small brush and cover them with a finishing coat like Model Magic Glossy Glaze.
- Your model doesn't need to be made entirely of modeling compound. Dress it up with a wig, or give it accessories like glasses or earrings.
- Try using Tinkercad to create a 3D model of your face that you can print out on a 3D printer. You can upload a 2D image to Tinkercad and build it up, the same way you would with clay.

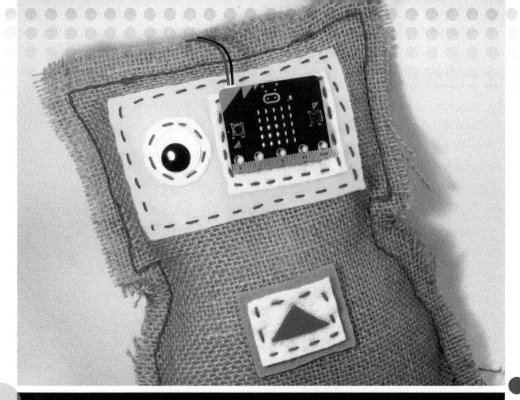

# Project: Make a Sewable Programmable FiberBot

**TURN A CUTE RAGDOLL INTO A CYBORG WITH ELECTRONICS THAT ADD SENSORS, SOUND, AND ANIMATION.**

Amazingly, one way to keep robots from falling into the Uncanny Valley is to make them look goofy. Research has shown that the simple addition of googly eyes will make a machine-shaped robot more likable.

In 2019, a library in Helsinki, Finland, decided to transform its book-shelving robots into guides that could help visitors find the section they were looking for. But people didn't know how to interact with the robots, which looked like rolling boxes.

When they gave the bots some happy chirps and little spinning movements that let visitors know they were ready to lead the way, the robots became much more popular. But what really made a difference was slapping some giant googly eyes on the front of the machines. When people knew they were looking at the "face" of the robot, they could anticipate which way it was going to start moving.

That same year, Giant Food Stores brought in 300 customer-assistance robots named Marty to their supermarkets along the East Coast. The giant-sized machines — taller than the average human — were designed to detect spills and alert store employees to problems in the aisles. Even though they used a laser-based detection system to find their way around, the stores added oversized googly eyes to make the robots feel less threatening.

Cartoon faces can help big hard-bodied robots look more friendly. But giving a robot a soft, cushy body can work too. Paro is a robotic baby seal with a huggable fuzzy body that reacts with coos and wiggles when it is petted and held. Invented by Takanori Shibata, the chief senior research scientist at Japan's National Institute of Advanced Industrial Science and Technology, Paro has sensors that help it respond to touch, light, and sound. To avoid the Uncanny Valley, Shibata chose an animal that people were unlikely to have met in real life. Paro has been used around the world as a therapy robot for older people with memory problems. Studies show that spending an hour touching and holding Paro can reduce patients' pain and lift their spirits.

In this project, you'll create a cuddly *cyborg* – a combination of a normal body with robotic parts. In this case, the body belongs to a stuffed doll you will make by sewing a pattern that's simple enough for beginning stitchers. Then, to turn it into a real robot, you'll attach a mini-computer called the BBC micro:bit, and program it in a block-based software language called Microsoft MakeCode. The micro:bit will let you add two elements to make the robot seem even friendlier: an interactive digital googly eye that moves when you tilt the robot (along with a real googly eye), and a beepy-boopy voice that responds when you talk to it.

# Meet micro:bit

The BBC micro:bit is a pocket-sized computer originally developed by a group of tech organizations in the UK to teach young people how software (computer code) and hardware (electronic parts) work together. In 2016, the tiny boards were sent out to nearly a million 11- and 12-year-old students in Great Britain. Today, there are more than 5 million micro:bits in use around the world.

The micro:bit board holds a microcontroller that can run several types of software (including Scratch!). It also has a variety of input and output components that can take information in and interact with the outside world. A new version released in 2020 adds even more features, but you can still use the older version. A quick tour of the micro:bit board includes:

- A 5 by 5 grid of red LED lights that can scroll words and numbers and display animations

- Sensors to record information:
  - two input buttons
  - an accelerometer that can measure tilt and speed
  - a compass to indicate direction
  - the LED grid can be used like a sensor to detect light levels

- Five pins (connector rings):
  - Pins 0, 1, and 2 are for connecting input and output devices (including ones you build yourself)
  - Pin 3V (3 volts) sends power to an external device, like a motor
  - Pin GND is a ground (for completing a circuit)

- Sockets for plugging in:
  - a microUSB cable for uploading and downloading information to your computer
  - a connector for a battery pack (usually two AA batteries or a 3V coin battery)

- Bluetooth for sending signals and code back and forth with another micro:bit or other Bluetooth-enabled device

- A 25-pin edge connector that lets you expand what the board can do (using add-on breakout boards that are sold separately)

The micro:bit v2 (version 2) also has extra built-in abilities:
- Additional input and output:
  - a microphone (sound sensor) with its own LED
  - a speaker to play sounds you program in
  - a touch sensor on the board's logo
  - a temperature sensor

- Sleep mode — hold down the reset button until the power LED goes out to save on batteries

**TIP:** You can find a ton of information, lessons, and ideas on the micro:bit website: microbit.org.

## WHAT TO EXPECT

- **Time Needed:** 3–4 hours (less for experienced robot builders; more if you're a newbie)
- **Cost:** $30–$40 (including reusable electronics)
- **Difficulty:** Moderate
- **Safety Issues:** Use care with batteries around young children.

## SKILLS YOU WILL USE

- Sewing and stuffing a soft robot body
- Attaching electronics to fabric
- Programming basics, including conditional statements
- Working with MakeCode
- Downloading a MakeCode program to the micro:bit

## ELECTRONICS SUPPLIES

- micro:bit v2 microcontroller (v1 will also work, but won't include sound)
- USB data cable with a USB micro B plug and an end that fits your computer
- Optional: battery pack for the micro:bit (preferably a pack that holds 2 AA batteries and has an on/off switch)

## CRAFT SUPPLIES

- FiberBot template (or draw your own pattern)
- Fabric that's easy to work with, such as felt, fleece, denim, or burlap — about 1 by 2 feet (30 by 60 centimeters), or two separate pieces that are each about 1 square foot (30 square centimeters)
- Felt, two or more colors (peel-and-stick felt can be used to eliminate some of the sewing)
- Embroidery yarn (also called craft yarn, less glossy than embroidery floss)
- Wide needle with an eye large enough for a full strand of embroidery yarn, such as a tapestry needle (with a rounded point) or embroidery needle (with a sharp point)
- 1 large googly eye (or other kind of eye, such as a button)

- Cardstock (as a backing for the micro:bit)
- Fiberfill stuffing for the body (you can also use fabric scraps or dryer lint)
- Peel-and-stick fabric adhesive sheets (the no-iron type)
- Masking tape (or duct tape) to attach the micro:bit board to its holder
- Peel-and-stick Velcro tape or dots to attach the battery pack to the fabric

## INSTRUCTIONS FOR THE FIBERBOT BODY

1. To use the design shown in these instructions as a sewing pattern:
   - Copy and print out the design onto regular-sized printer paper. Enlarge the design to at least 9 1/2 inches (24 centimeters) high, so the googly eye and the micro:bit board will fit on the face (Figure Ⓐ).

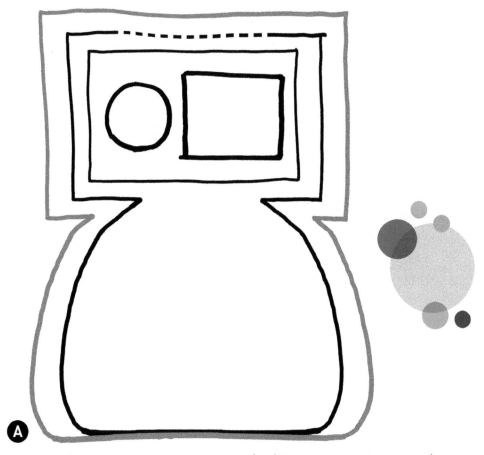

Ⓐ

(Downloadable template: makezine.com/go/simple-robot-templates)

**B**

- Cut out the pattern. Be sure to include the **seam allowance**, which is the space between the **seam** (the line you will sew along) and the edge you cut out of fabric.
- Take a double layer of fabric as big as your pattern. If you need to, use clips or straight pins to hold the layers together.
- Place the pattern on the fabric. If you are using one long piece folded in half, the bottom seam line — *not* the seam allowance line — goes right along the fold.
- Trace around the pattern onto the fabric with a soft pencil (Figure **B**). ***Also mark the opening in the seam at the top***. This is where you will insert the stuffing.
- Remove the paper pattern, and cut out along the pencil line you drew, going through both layers of fabric.

2. Next, to make the face:
   - Cut the large face rectangle out of the paper pattern. Transfer it to a piece of felt the same way you did with the body and cut a single layer of felt. You do not need a seam allowance (Figure **C**).
   - Cut out the smaller rectangle and the circle from the paper, and use them to cut out felt pieces the same way.
   - Use small pieces of peel-and-stick fabric adhesive to attach the felt

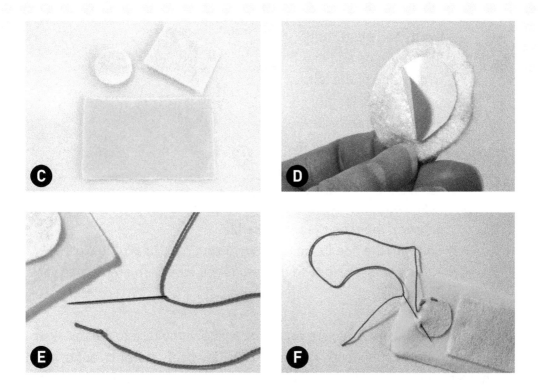

pieces to the face. If you also want to stitch around the outside, keep the adhesive away from the edges where you plan to sew (Figure **D**). (It's very hard to push a needle through the glue.)

- To sew around the felt pieces with a running (in-and-out) stitch (Figure **E**):
  - Take a piece of embroidery yarn no longer than your arm. (Do not separate it into strands.) Thread it through the eye of the needle. Make a knot at the longer end of the thread. Leave the shorter end loose (but hold onto it as you sew so it doesn't slip out of the needle's eye.)
  - Your stitches will go in a line near the edge. Use a stitch length of about 1/4 inch (3 millimeters). Start with the needle at the wrong side of the fabric (Figure **F**). (In sewing terms, the wrong side of the fabric is the side you won't see when the piece is finished. The right side is the side that shows.) Poke the needle through to the right side. Go one stitch length along the stitching line. Then poke the needle down through to the wrong side. Pull

the thread gently until the knot is up against the wrong side of the felt.

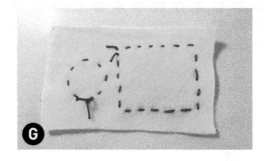

- Go one stitch length along the wrong side and bring the needle up through to the right side again. Continue to sew in and out, all around the edge. Keep the stitches and the spaces between them as even as possible.
- End with the needle going down through to the wrong side. Make a knot as close to the felt as you can. Trim any excess yarn (Figure **G**).

3. When the smaller pieces are on the face, attach the face to the top layer of fabric for the robot body the same way. Use peel-and-stick adhesive to hold it in place, and then sew around the edge if you choose (Figure **H**).

4. Now sew the two layers of the FiberBot body together along the seam. (Don't forget to leave the opening for the stuffing!) The seam allowance stays on the outside. If you are using a fabric with a loose weave like burlap, be careful not to let it unravel too much. This time, use a backstitch to lock the stitches and help keep the stuffing inside:
   - Line up the front and back layers, with the felt facing up towards you. Use clips or straight pins if you need help keeping the layers together.
   - Thread the needle, but don't knot the yarn. Begin at one side of the opening along the top of the robot's head. To hide the tail of the yarn, start on the wrong side of the fabric (between the two layers) and bring the needle through to the right side of the front. Take one stitch **through both layers together**. Then anchor the stitch by going over the same place three times. (Anchor the beginning and end of every piece of yarn the same way.) End with the needle at the back of the robot (Figure **I**).

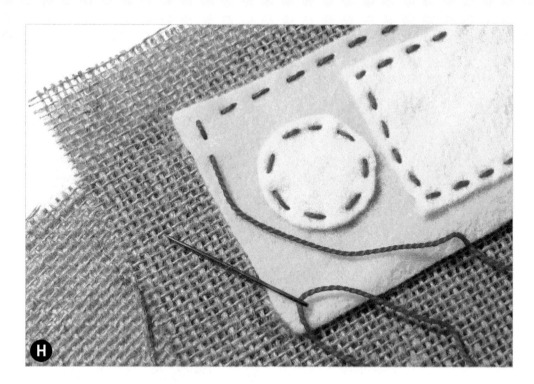

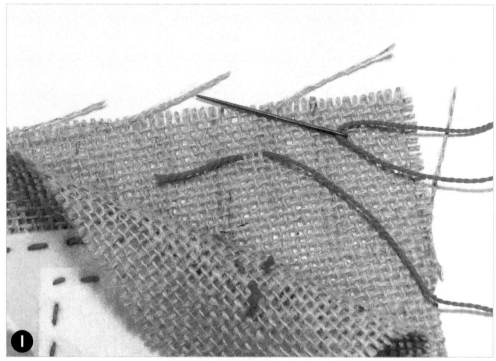

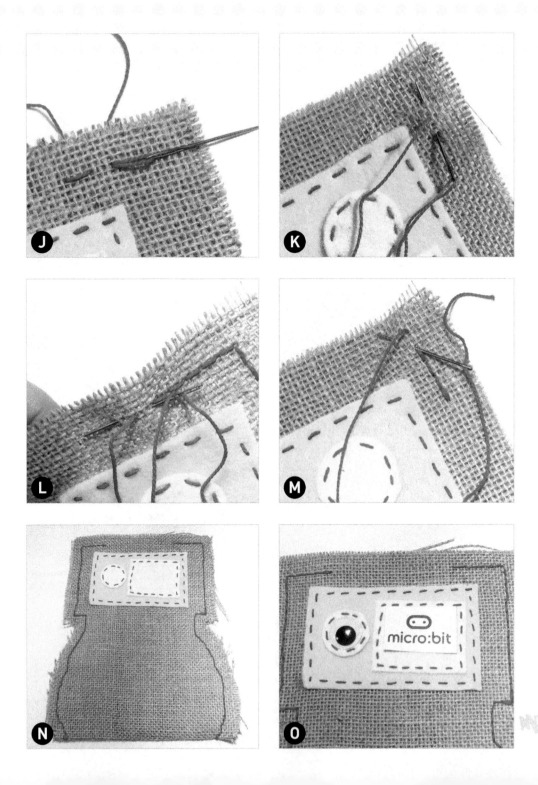

- Now go one stitch length away and bring the needle up through to the front (Figure **J**).
- From the front, loop back to the end of the last stitch and bring the needle down to the back, filling the empty space (Figure **K**).
- For the next stitch, do the same thing: Go one stitch length ahead, bring the needle up from back to front, loop back to the end of the last stitch, bring the needle down through to the back and fill the empty stitch (Figure **L**).
- Continue on down the first side. Where the stitching turns a corner, you can reinforce it by going over the stitches twice (Figure **M**).
- When you reach the bottom — the fold — stop and anchor the thread. Then bring the needle between the two layers and out again. Cut the yarn. Repeat to sew the other side closed (Figure **N**). (If you have two separate pieces of fabric, sew across the bottom and up the other side, stopping at the opening.)

5. Before stuffing the body, finish off the face:
   - Attach the googly eye to the felt circle with fabric adhesive (Figure **O**).
   - To keep the felt from muffling the speaker on the back of the micro:bit v2, make a cardstock backing. The backing also makes it easier to attach and remove the micro:bit. Here's how:
     - Trace around the micro:bit on the smaller felt rectangle.
     - Cut a rectangle of cardstock about 2 inches (5 centimeters) long by 1 1/2 inches (4 centimeters) wide. This is shorter than the micro:bit, so you can still attach clips to the pins along the bottom.
     - Use peel-and-stick fabric adhesive to attach the cardstock to the upper end of the felt rectangle where the micro:bit will go. That way, there's no backing behind the lower end of the board.

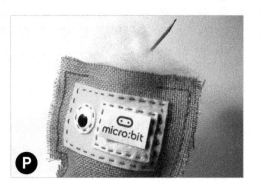

P

Q

R

S

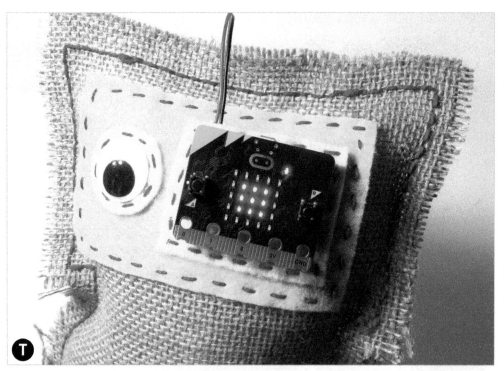

T

6. To add the stuffing:
   - Insert the stuffing into the FiberBot through the opening at the top of the head. Pack the stuffing in loosely. You want enough stuffing to give it a little thickness, but not so much that it strains or tears the fabric. Use the eraser end of a pencil, a chopstick, or the handle of a wood spoon to get the stuffing into any corners you can't reach with your fingers (Figure **P**).
   - Close up the opening with a backstitch (Figure **Q**).

7. Time to connect the electronics! To attach the micro:bit:
   - Take about 2 inches of masking tape and roll it into a tube, sticky side out. Make a second tape tube the same way (Figure **R**).
   - Take the sticky tape tubes and attach them to the back of the micro:bit, along the sides.
   - Press the micro:bit with the tape onto the cardstock. Make sure there's a little space between the board and the cardstock.

8. To connect the battery pack:
   - Plug the battery pack into the micro:bit using the JST connector. Don't put in batteries yet!
   - Stick a piece of peel-and-stick Velcro on the bottom of the battery case, opposite the side with the on/off switch. Stick the matching piece of Velcro to the FiberBot's back (or wherever you want to attach the battery case). Press firmly so the adhesive adheres to the fabric (Figure **S**).
   - Tip: If you ever have trouble unplugging the JST plug, use a pair of pliers to gently pull it out of the socket.

9. The body is done (Figure **T**). You're ready to code the micro:bit!

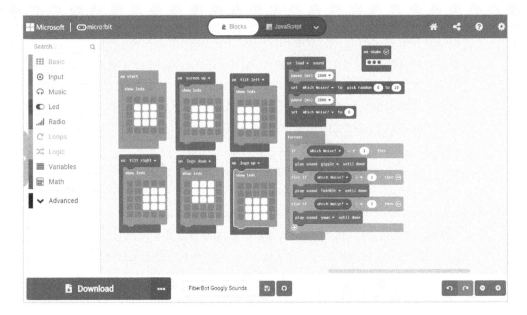

# INSTRUCTIONS FOR CODING THE MICRO:BIT WITH MAKECODE

To see and edit the sample code shown here, go to makecode.microbit.org/_7TwTC026rixJ. Click "Edit" to open the code in the MakeCode workspace so you can try it out.

This program makes the digital "googly eye" roll around, depending on how you tilt it (or shake it). At the same time, it plays one of three random sounds if you speak loudly or clap.

# MakeCode Basics

MakeCode is a free block-based programming language created by Microsoft to help students learn coding. It looks and feels very much like MIT's Scratch, the software you used in Chapter 3. The biggest difference is that your program runs on an on-screen simulation as you build it. You can program lights to flash when you push a button, or music to play when the board shakes, and watch the animated simulation to see if you got everything right. You don't need to download MakeCode to your computer. Build your program in your web browser, then download it to the micro:bit board. There's also a MakeCode Offline App that works on computers running Windows or Mac OS.

Here's how to get started programming in MakeCode:

- **Check out the MakeCode micro:bit website** (makecode.microbit. org). There are tutorials and sample projects on the main page to help you get started.

- **To begin, click New Project.** You don't need an account to use MakeCode. Just give the new project a name and start working. To save a program you write, you "publish" it to the MakeCode site. That creates a link you can go back to later from any device, or share with friends. (If you change the program, you have to save it again and create a new link.)

- **To "remix" an existing program, just give it a new name.** Type over the old name in the space at the bottom of the editing screen before you save it.

- **See what's inside the editing page.** Just like Scratch, MakeCode has three main sections:
  - In the middle, there's a column of different colors and categories of blocks to choose from that looks much like the Blocks Palette in Scratch. (In MakeCode, it's called the toolbox.) Click on "Advanced" at the bottom of the column to reveal more categories. Click on "Extensions" to open a page with even more categories.
  - On the right, the programming canvas/editor is the workspace for putting blocks of code together.
  - On the left, the micro:bit simulator runs automatically anytime you make a change to your program. To test a reaction to a button press or logo touch, click on the object right on the simulation. When you program a sensor, a sliding scale appears that you can test by moving it up and down.
  - In the top right of the screen are icons for creating a link to share your program, accessing the Help menu, and adjusting the Settings.
  - At the top, in the center of the screen, is a slider that lets you switch between Blocks and written code. You have a choice of two text languages to work in: JavaScript, which is what most websites are built with, and Python, a language used with many microcontroller boards.

- On the bottom, from left to right:
    - a Download button for transferring your program to your micro:bit
    - a space for giving your program a name
    - an icon for saving the program directly to your computer
    - an Undo button
    - buttons to zoom in or out

- **Just like Scratch, you can start to write your program by stacking blocks.**
    - The "on start" and "forever" blocks are already in the workspace when you create a new project.
    - Click on a category to find and drag a block into the workspace in the middle. For some categories, a second line that says "more" will open up below the first with more choices. Some useful categories are:
        - **Basic:** Some blocks to let you program animations and scrolling letters and numbers on the LED grid. You'll also find the "forever," "pause," and "on start" blocks here.
        - **Input:** Blocks that start an action based on readings from the micro:bit's sensors and buttons.
        - **Music:** Blocks to create your own melody or choose a pre-made one. There are some fun sound effects further down in this menu.
        - **Loops:** Different ways to make a piece of programming run multiple times, including "repeat" and "while."
        - **Logic:** Conditional blocks, such as "if-then-else," and comparison blocks for numbers, letters, and sensor readings.

- **The blocks work pretty much the same way as in Scratch:**
    - Add more blocks below the first to make them snap together.
    - To move a stack of connected blocks, grab the top block.
    - To copy a block or stack of blocks, right click on the top block,

then click "Duplicate."
- Pull a stack of blocks apart from underneath.
- To delete a block, drag it over the column of block categories.
- You can type words or numbers right into an oval-shaped white space.
- You can drag pointy-ended or oval-shaped blocks into the same shape spaces on other blocks to make them snap into place.

- **To download your MakeCode program to your micro:bit, connect the board to your computer with a micro USB data cable.** (Be sure to use a data cable. A regular charging cable won't work!) For more tips, see the box "**How to Download MakeCode to the micro:bit**" on page 139.

1. The FiberBot Googly Sounds sample program we will build does three things:
   - It makes the LED "googly eye" animation move in the direction you tilt it.
   - It makes the eye roll around if you shake it.
   - It plays one of three random robot sounds if you speak to it or make another loud sound.

**The algorithm for the program might look like this:**
   - Check to see which way the micro:bit is facing. Also listen for a loud sound.
   - If the micro:bit is held facing the ceiling, show an "eye" in the center of the LED grid.
   - If the micro:bit is facing left, or right, move the "eye" to that side of the LED grid.
   - If the micro:bit is facing you, right side up, let the "eye" fall to the bottom of the grid. If it's upside down, let the "eye" slide to the top of the grid.

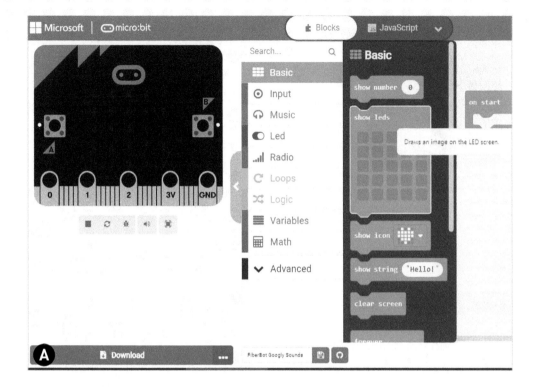

- If the micro:bit is shaken, make the "eye" roll around the outside of the LED grid.
- If the micro:bit detects a loud sound, pick a random number from 1–3.
- Play a different sound depending on the number picked.

Once you understand how it works, feel free to program in your own inputs, animations, and sounds!

2. Open MakeCode (makecode.microbit.org), click "New Project," and give it a name. The editing screen will open and you can begin to build your program.

3. Begin with the "on start" block that's already in your workspace (Figure Ⓐ). To make sure your micro:bit googly eye is always in the center when you turn it on:

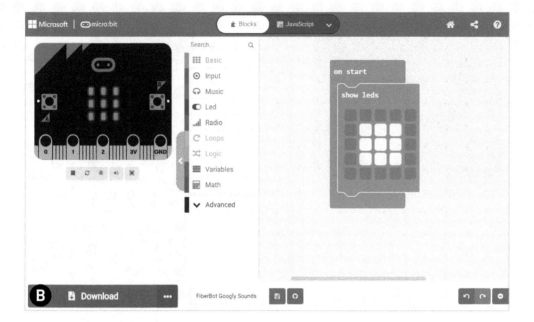

- Open the Basic menu (blue).
- Drag a "show leds" block inside the "on start" block (Figure **B**).
- Draw the eye by clicking on the lights in the grid to turn them on. The eye in the example is a square of 3 by 3 lights, right in the middle of the grid.

4. You will need a lot of eye images for this project, so right click on the "show leds" block and duplicate it. It will look gray and see-through, like a ghost, until you add it to a stack that tells it when to run (Figure **C**).

5. To make the micro:bit eye move around just like the real googly eye (Figure **D**):
   - Open the Input menu and drag the "on [shake]" block into the workspace.
   - Snap it around the duplicate "show leds" block.
   - Click on the little triangle-arrow next to the word "shake" to open a drop-down menu of different conditions measured by the tilt sensor (the accelerometer) (Figure **E**).

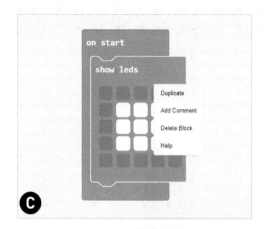

**C**

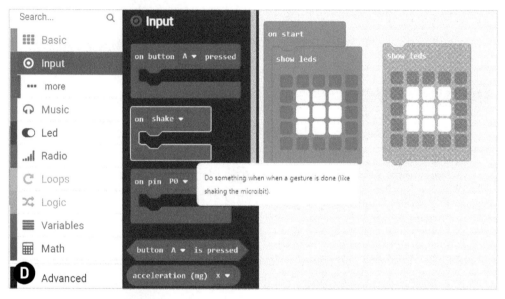

on button A ▼ pressed

on shake ▼

on pin P0 ▼

Do something when when a gesture is done (like shaking the micro:bit).

button A ▼ is pressed

acceleration (mg) x ▼

Search...

Basic
Input
more
Music
Led
Radio
Loops
Logic
Variables
Math
Advanced

**D**

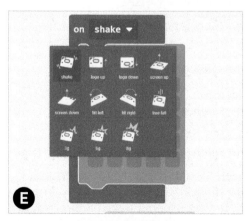

on shake ▼

shake · logo up · logo down · screen up
screen down · tilt left · tilt right · free fall
3g · 6g · 8g

**E**

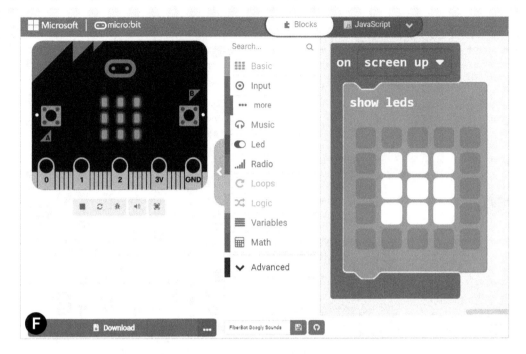

- Choose"screen up." When the FiberBot is in this position, it will face the ceiling, and the digital googly eye will be resting in the middle of the micro:bit's LED grid (Figure **F**). (You can check if the positions you program are correct by looking at how the real googly eye moves around!).

6. Now, to make the eye move when you tilt the board:
   - Right click on the outer "on screen up" block and duplicate the entire mini-stack. It will also look like a ghost, because you already have a block that says "screen up." So change it to another choice: "tilt left" (Figure **G**).
   - To move the eye to the left, click on the lights you need to turn on. Then click on the already-lit LED squares you need to turn off. In this case, you will turn on the column of lights next to the left side of the eye, and turn off the lights on the right side.
   - Stop and test your program on the micro:bit simulation. Notice that if you mouse over or click on the left side of the simulated board, the animation tilts to the left. Does the eye design move to the left?

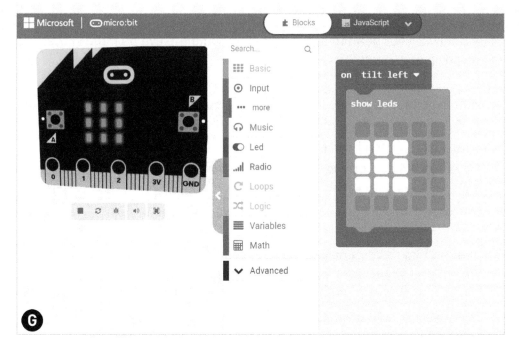

Does it go back to the middle when you let the board go flat again? If it does, then your code is working!

- Follow the same steps to make the eye move in other directions (Figure **H**):
  - tilt right
  - logo down (the logo is the little oval face at the top of the micro:bit, so "logo down" means the FiberBot is standing on its head.
  - logo up.

If you want to, you can also do "screen down," but you'd have to hold the FiberBot over your head to see it! (Where should the eye be if the screen points straight down?)

7. At this point, the googly eye motion is complete! Before moving onto some sillier animated moves, stop and download the code to your micro:bit to watch how it works on the real thing! See the "**How to Download MakeCode to the micro:bit**" box on page 139 for instructions. You can work with the micro:bit right on the FiberBot. If the masking tape loses its grip, just replace it when you're done.

8. Just for fun, create another stack of code that makes the googly eye roll around when you shake the robot. To do that, you'll stack a series of "show leds" blocks. When the program runs, the blocks will act like the frames of an animated film — as they appear one after the other, it will look like the eye is moving! Here's what to do:
   - Duplicate the "on [screen up]" block again, with the "show leds" block that displays the eye in the middle of the grid. This time, change the movement back to "shake" (Figure 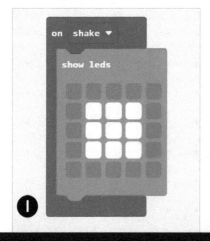).
   - Now duplicate just the "show leds" block. Drag the duplicate right below the first block, inside the mouth of the "on [shake]" block. The mouth will open wider as you add more blocks. Change the lights on the second block to show the eye at the bottom of the grid (Figure 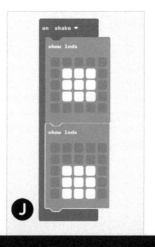).

# How to Download MakeCode to the micro:bit

1. The file type for micro:bit programs ends with a ".hex" suffix. The basic steps to download the .hex code to your board are:

   - Plug a USB data cable into the micro:bit and your computer.
   - Click the purple "Download" button on the bottom left of the MakeCode screen).
   - Move the .hex file from your computer onto the micro:bit drive.For instructions on how to download a MakeCode program with your browser, check out makecode.microbit.org/device/usb.) The example here shows what to do if you use a Chrome browser:
     - Look for the file name at the bottom of your browser window.
     - Click the V-arrow next to the file name to make a menu pop up. Choose "Show in folder."
     - Open the file explorer on your computer. The .hex file may appear in the Downloads folder.

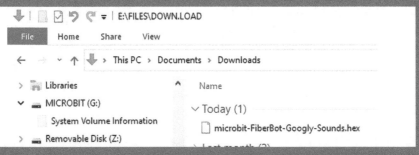

- Look for a drive on your computer labeled MICROBIT. Drag the .hex file (or copy and paste it) to the MICROBIT drive. That's it! A light on the micro:bit board will pulse on and off for a few seconds, and then the program should start to run.

**NOTE:** On some computers, you can "pair" the board so that .hex files move to the micro:bit automatically. This is a handy shortcut, but it's not a good idea if you also like to save the .hex files to another folder on your computer. To set up the pairing option, look for the instructions on the "Download Complete" pop-up box that appears after you copy your program to the computer.

- Duplicate and move the second block the same way. Change the lights to show the eye in the bottom left corner (Figure **K**).
- Keep going, duplicating the blocks and moving the eye all around the grid. End with the eye in the middle again (Figure **L**).
- Test your program by "shaking" the simulated micro:bit on the screen. Then download it to the real board to see how it looks. Make any changes you think it needs (Figure **M**).
- At this point, your stack of blocks is pretty long! To tidy it up, right click on the "on [shake]" block. When the menu pops up, choose

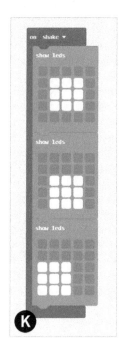
**K**

**L**

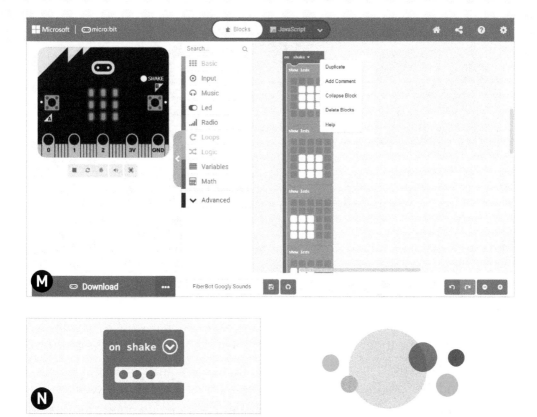

"Collapse Block." The whole stack will shrink down to just the purple "on [shake]" block with three dots inside. Click the arrow to open up the whole stack again (Figure **N**).

9.  Now give the FiberBot even more personality by making it talk! Write another stack of code that tells the micro:bit to listen for a voice or sound, and then "answer" with random robot noises. To do all that, you will program the micro:bit to:
    *   Wait before it responds when it hears a loud noise, like a voice (so the person has a chance to finish speaking).
    *   Pick a random number.
    *   Select which robot noise to make, based on what number it picks!

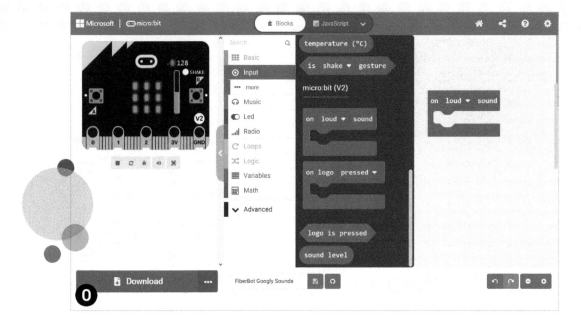

10. First, go to the Input menu (light purple) and scroll down to the bottom (Figure **0**). Then:
    - Find the "on [loud] sound" block and drag it into the workspace.
    - Notice that a little image of a microphone lights up on the simulated board. This means you have turned on the sound sensor.
    - Next to the light is the number 128, and below that is a scale that looks like a thermometer. These show what sound level is being detected by the sound sensor. The numbers go from 0 to 255, so 128 is in the middle. You will use these later to test the sound part of your program.

11. To make the robot wait before it responds to a voice or sound:
    - Go to the Basic menu (blue), and scroll down to find a "pause (ms) [100]" block.
    - Drag it into the "on [loud] sound" block.
    - The length of the pause is measured in milliseconds (written as "ms"). One thousand milliseconds equals 1 second (Figure **P**). To make the pause longer:
        - Click on the arrow next to the "100" to open a menu.

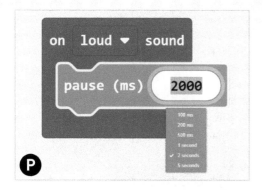

P

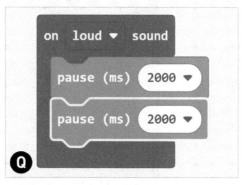

Q

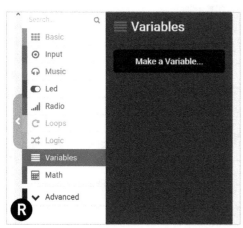

R

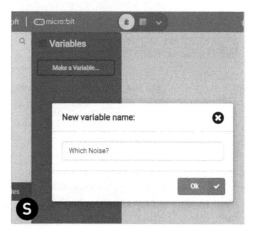

S

- Choose "2 seconds," or 2,000ms (Figure Q). (You can adjust this later, when you test the program.)

12. To pick a random number that tells the robot which noise to make, you need a **variable**. A variable is used in computer programming and in math equations to stand for a piece of information (such as a number) that can change at different times. (You already used a kind of variable block in Scratch, a counter that went up every time it ran.) To create a variable:
    - Open the Variables menu (red). Click on "Make a Variable..." (Figure R).
    - Give your variable a name by typing it in the box (Figure S). The name should describe what it stands for, such as "Which Noise?"
    - Blocks will appear with the name of the variable you have created.

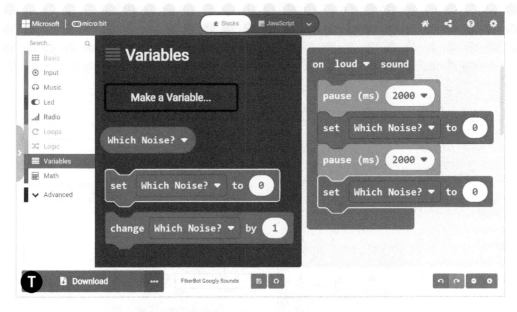

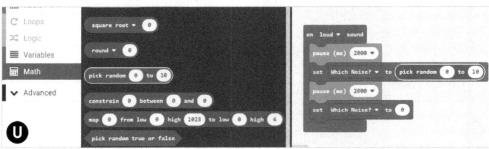

Drag a "set [Which Noise?] to [0]" block inside the "on [loud] sound" block. Make a duplicate, and stack it underneath the first (Figure **T**).

- Duplicate the pause block, and drag it between the variable blocks. This will give the program time to pick a random number, then set the variable back to zero so it doesn't keep playing over and over.
- Go back to the first variable block. In the Math menu (purple), scroll down to find the "pick random [0] to [10]" block (Figure **U**). It's oval-shaped.
- Drag the "random" block over the oval space on the variable block. To make it easier, MakeCode will join the block to the space with little red dots and a line between them (Figure **V**).
- Set the numbers in the random block to 1 and 3. This will let you have the robot play up to three different noises (Figure **W**). (You can change the number to add more!)

**13.** Finally, create one more stack of blocks to help the robot decide which noise to play. It will use an "if-then-else" block to tell the micro:bit what to do when the variable is set to 1, 2, or 3. The steps are:

- Find the "forever" block that was there when you opened the project. If you can't find it, grab a new one from the Basic menu (blue).
- Go to the Logic menu (teal, a kind of dark greenish-blue). From the Conditionals section, drag an "if [true] then" block into the "forever" block (Figure **X**). (It doesn't matter whether you use the block with or without the "else" mouth — you can always click on the plus and minus icons on the block to add or delete an "else.")

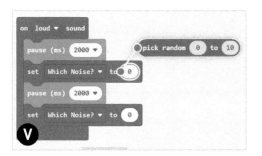

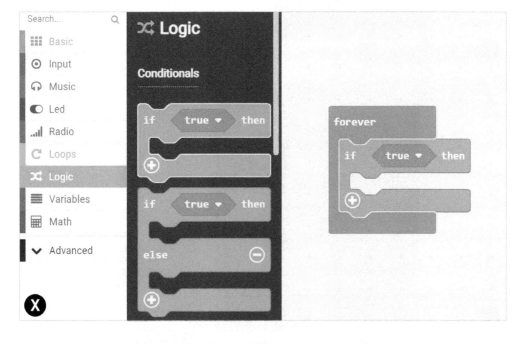

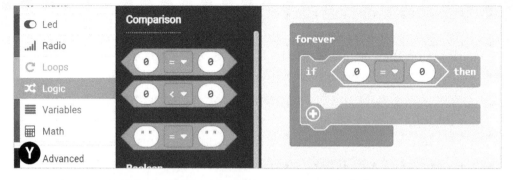

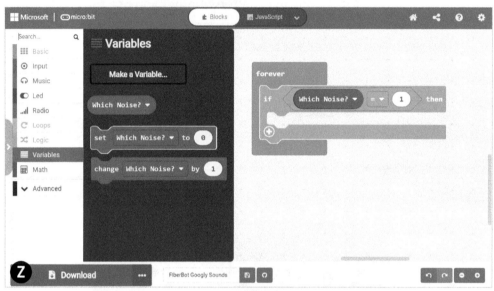

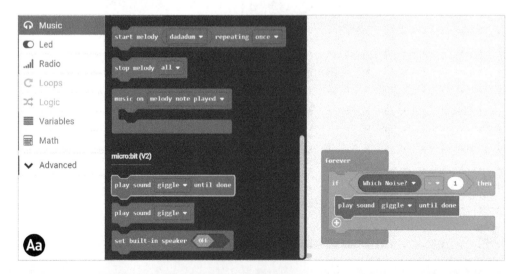

- Go back to the Logic menu. From the Comparison section, drag the "[0 = 0]" block with the pointy ends into the "true" space on the "if-then" block (Figure 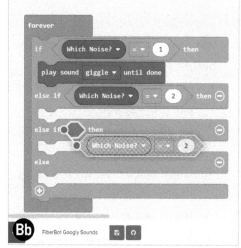).
- From the Variable menu (red), drag an oval-shaped block into the first oval space on the Comparison block. Make sure it has the same name as the variable you created before. Type the number 1 into the other space (Figure **Z**).
- To choose a robot noise, open the Music menu (orange) and scroll down to find the "play sound [giggle] until done" block. Drag it into the mouth of the "if-then" block (Figure **Aa**).
- For numbers 2 and 3, repeat the same set-up using the "else" line (Figure **Bb**):
  - To make the next "else" line and mouth appear, click on the plus sign on the bottom of the "forever" block.
  - Duplicate the pointy-ended Comparison block, insert it into the next open mouth, and type in the new number.
  - Duplicate the "play sound" block and insert it into the mouth.
  - To close the last mouth, click on the minus sign.

**Bb** FiberBot Googly Sounds

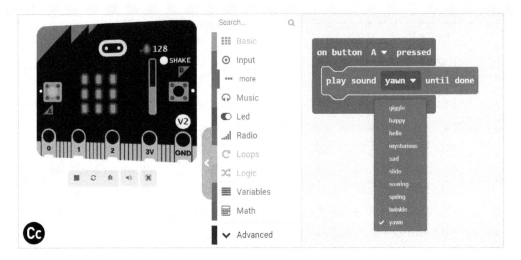

Cc

**14.** Choose three different sounds for your three random numbers (Figure **Cc**). If you want to hear what they sound like first, set up a quick stack of blocks to test them out:

- Go to Input (violet) and drag an "on button [A] pressed" block into the workspace.
- Duplicate a "play sound" block and insert it into the mouth of the button block.
- Click the arrow on the "play sound" block to show the drop-down menu of different sounds. Then just pick a sound name and click on the A button on the micro:bit simulation to hear what it sounds like.

**15.** When you're finished, you will have an "if-then-else-else" stack of three numbers and three sounds (Figure **Dd**).

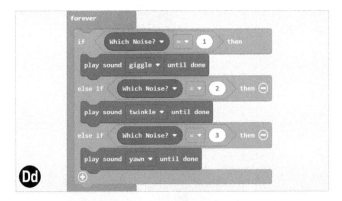

Dd

## GO BEYOND

- Using conductive tape, give your soft robot some felt buttons that respond to touch, and connect them to the micro:bit with alligator clip wires. Look at the Guitar Touch Tunes project on the micro:bit site to see how it works: microbit.org/projects/make-it-code-it/guitar-1-touch-tunes. Also see my book *Fabric and Fiber Inventions* for other kinds of sensors you can build from felt and conductive tape or thread.

- The micro:bit doesn't have a light sensor, but you can use its built-in LEDs to detect light levels. Write a program that makes your robot blink when you shine a light at it, or let out a startled squeak when a shadow falls over it.

- Turn your FiberBot into a chatbot by programming the micro:bit to respond to questions with scrolling sentences on its LED grid. Use the random command to make it display general yes/no answers when it hears a sound. Or, for more advanced software engineers, there are also some machine learning speech recognition programs that can run on the micro:bit!

**NOTE:** You can see video of this project on my website at kathyceceri.com/making-simple-robots.

# #5

# MAKING ROBOTS PLAYFUL

Invent **fun**, **artsy robots** with engineering, coding, and a little imagination!

With their machine bodies and computer brains, robots can be very precise. But that doesn't mean they don't like to play and be creative!

Robots that make their own art give everyday things a unique twist. Ai-Da is a realistic-looking "robot artist" who creates drawings with the help of camera eyes and an AI brain. The robot was the idea of Aidan Meller and Lucy Seal of Oxford University in Britain, and was built by Engineered Arts in 2019. A team of programmers, roboticists, art experts, and psychologists worked on Ai-Da's design, and the self-portraits she produces combine photography, drawing, painting, and more. Ai-Da was named after Ada Lovelace, who, in the 1800s — long before computers and electronics existed — came up with the idea of programming machines to do more than solve math problems.

But robots don't have to be super-advanced to be artists. They can even be works of art themselves! As you saw with the Scratch chatbot in Chapter 3, adding some random moves to a robot's behavior can make it seem more lifelike, like it has a mind of its own. In 1991, robotics physicist Mark W. Tilden came up with the idea for a style of robot that moves in random bursts of activity. He called it BEAM robotics, which stands for Biology, Electronics, Aesthetics (meaning "beauty"), and Mechanics.

*The author's version of BEAM robots, with some non-BEAM-like messy wires left showing.*

All BEAM robots are solar powered. They are designed to move after they have stored up enough energy from the sun. That design lets them interact with their environment by reflex instead of high-level thinking. Their "nervous system" is made of old-fashioned switches and transistors, instead of a circuit board with a built-in computer "brain." But that doesn't mean they look like a mess of loose wires and duct tape. The parts of a BEAM robot fit together into one neat shape, just like a living organism. In fact, many BEAM robots resemble solar-powered insects.

BEAM inspired the Hexbug line of bug-like micro robotic toys that includes walkers, crawlers, and little vibrating Hexbug Nanos. Hexbugs are real robots, with motors, sensors, and electronics (or, in the case of Nanos, programmable bodies) that tell them which direction to go in. They are made by Innovation First International, the company that also produces VEX Robotics kits for education and competition.

In this chapter you'll build playful programmable robots that only use a few moving parts. The Pen-Propelled DrawBot moves by swinging the weight of a marker from side to side, creating different artwork every time. Can you figure out how to steer it by controlling the movements of its pen? You'll also make String Straw HexaWalker, a fun little hexapod (six-legged) robot that looks like a tensegrity but ambles along like an insect. Watch out — these robots may be small, but they'll surprise you with their big personalities!

*Two of the six-legged style of Hexbug.*

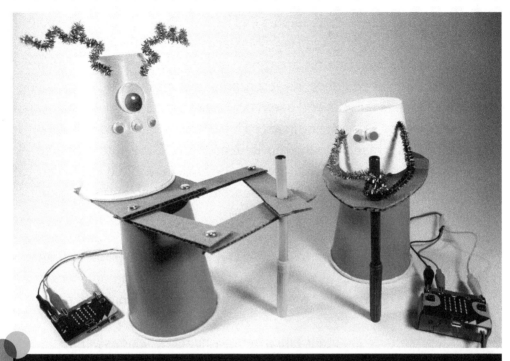

# Project: Make a Pen-Propelled DrawBot

**STEER A DRAWING ROBOT AROUND WITH A SERVO TO MOVE THE PEN AND A MICRO:BIT TILT CONTROLLER.**

Robots that can write and draw have been around for a long, long time. Even before the age of electricity, there were automata, which are contraptions that can move thanks to springs, cranks, cables, and weights.

In the late 1700s, watchmaker Pierre Jaquet-Droz built several automata that still work today. They include a mechanical boy that writes as many as 40 different letters and characters, and another that draws different pictures. As they work, their eyes follow the movement of their hand across the page, and they stop to dip their quills in an inkwell. To program them, their operators arrange a series of removable teeth that turn different gears on and off inside. Visitors enjoy watching the automata in action at the Neuchâtel Museum of Art and History in Switzerland.

The Franklin Institute in Philadelphia has its own drawing boy. It was built by another Swiss clock maker, Henri Maillardet, around the same time as the other automatons. But this amazing machine has the largest memory of any automaton in existence. Its "programs" include drawings of a sailing ship and a Chinese temple, and poems in French and English. Author Brian Selznick has said the boy inspired his book *The Invention of Hugo Cabret*, which was made into the movie *Hugo*. In 2007, the author helped the museum hire experts to put the machine back in working order. You can still see demonstrations of the Maillardet Automaton at the Franklin Institute today.

Drawing robots still exist, but today they look more like 3D printers than animatronic dolls. Known as a ***plotter***, this type of programmable writer usually has rails or arms that move a pen holder across a piece of paper.

Sometimes, plotters use other kinds of drawing tools besides pens. In 2013, a 12-year-old kid named Zephyrus Todd invented a plotter called WaterColorBot that used a brush and paint. It could copy paintings you programmed in, or follow your hand as you drew in a computer graphics program in real time. Todd exhibited the WaterColorBot at Maker Faires around the country, and at the White House Science Fair hosted by President Obama.

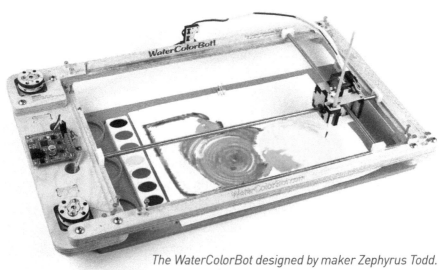

*The WaterColorBot designed by maker Zephyrus Todd.*

Evil Mad Scientist/WaterColorBot.com

There are even plotters that draw with food! PancakeBot was created by Miguel Valenzuela for his daughters. The first prototype was made with a LEGO Mindstorms Robotics kit. It squirted pancake batter from computer-controlled ketchup bottles onto a hot griddle to create tasty hotcakes shaped like rocket ships, buildings, animals, and more. Today, Lily, Maia, and Charlotte help their dad demonstrate factory-made PancakeBot machines at schools and maker events. (You can find Miguel's instructions for building a real working hand-powered food printer from LEGO bricks in my book *Edible Inventions*.)

PancakeBot

A much simpler style of drawing robot travels across a sheet of paper by vibration. Like the Tensegrity Robot in Chapter 2, it doesn't have an electronic brain. Instead, it has a programmable body that gives you some control over how it moves.

The Pen-Propelled DrawBot project you will build in this chapter moves in ways that are partly random, and partly controlled. You will be using the micro:bit as a remote control, connected to a motor with a wire. As you tilt the micro:bit to the left or right, it tells the robot to swing its pen around in the same direction. As the pen whips around, it jiggles the robot enough to make it move across the paper.

Try creating different versions of the robot's body and code to see how it affects its movement. You can even give your DrawBot extendable arms, so you can vary the distance of the pen from the robot's body. See if you can figure out how to draw particular designs and steer your robotic strolling artist where you want it to go!

## WHAT TO EXPECT

- **Time Needed:** 2–3 hours (less for experienced robot builders; more if you're a newbie)
- **Cost:** $30–$40 (including re-usable electronics)
- **Difficulty:** Moderate
- **Safety Issues:** Use care with batteries around young children.

## SKILLS YOU WILL USE

- Connecting a servo to the micro:bit
- Working with MakeCode, including:
  - programming a servo
  - creating and using variables
  - using sensor readings to control output

## ELECTRONIC SUPPLIES

- micro:bit V2 microcontroller (v1 will also work, but won't include sound)
- USB data cable with a USB micro-B plug and an end that fits your computer
- Micro servo (positional, not continuous) — often labeled as 9g — with servo horns that snap onto the shaft, and a cable with a plug that takes male jumper wires
- 3 alligator clip-to-male jumper wires in different colors (preferably red, black or brown, and yellow or orange to match the servo wires)
- Optional:
  - extra-long USB data cable (3 feet or more), so your bot can move around while connected to the computer for power and updating the program
  - additional male-to-female jumper wires for longer distance remote control
  - battery pack for the micro:bit
    the punch-out cardboard battery pack holder that comes with some micro:bits is handy for holding the board and batteries together; print and cut out your own from the micro:bit site (microbit.org/get-started/user-guide/battery-pack-holder).

you can also get a larger pack that holds two AA batteries and
has an on/off switch

## CRAFT SUPPLIES
- Markers (preferably washable)
- Cups or other lightweight, cut-able containers for the robot body
  - for the lower half of the body, look for a cup about the same size
    or shorter than the marker
  - for the head and upper body, a small cup or container that won't
    make the robot so top-heavy that it tips over
- Corrugated cardboard (or other stiff cardboard) for the marker
  holder (the arms)
- Sharp pencil for marking openings and poking holes
- Tape (any kind, including masking, double-sided scrapbooking tape,
  or glue dots)
- Drawing paper (to cover the area where the bot is moving around).
  Use a stack of several sheets to keep the marker from bleeding
  through to your work surface.
- Decorations, such as:
  - googly eyes
  - pipe cleaners
  - stickers
  - felt pieces
- Scissors, craft knife, or other tool for cutting holes in the cups

## INSTRUCTIONS FOR BUILDING THE BODY AND CONNECTING THE ELECTRONICS

1. To make the robot body, start with the lower half:
   - Take the bottom cup and turn it upside down, so the bottom is now the top. Decide which side will be the front of the robot. Place the servo motor on top of the cup, with the shaft — the part that spins — facing the front (Figure Ⓐ).
   - Trace around the bottom of the servo (just the bottom, not the "shoulders" of the servo). Cut out the shape you traced. Use the sharp pencil to make a starter hole if needed. Also cut a small hole at the back of the cup, big enough for the plug on the servo wire to pass through (Figure Ⓑ).
   - Insert the servo, wire first, into the hole at the top of the cup. Make sure it fits snugly. If not, use tape to hold the motor in place (Figure Ⓒ).
   - Bring the wire out through the hole in the side.

2. Next, make a simple holder for the marker (see Go Beyond for other ideas):
   - Cut a piece of corrugated cardboard bigger than the top of the cup. It needs to hang over the edge of the cup and hold a marker far enough away that it doesn't bang into the cup. You can make it oval, like the example, or any shape you choose.
   - Take a sharp pencil and poke a hole for a marker at one end of the holder. Keep the hole small enough to hold the marker securely (Figure Ⓓ). (You can test the marker to see how it fits, but remove it before the next step.)
   - To attach the other end of the holder to the servo, take one of the servo horns — the little plastic shapes that snap onto the shaft of the servo — and tape it to the underside of the cardboard holder (Figure Ⓔ).
   - Press the servo horn onto the servo shaft, then test to make sure it works (Figure Ⓕ):
     - Check whether the arm can swing around from side to side

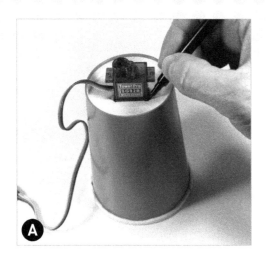

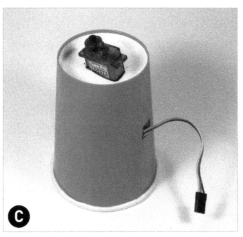

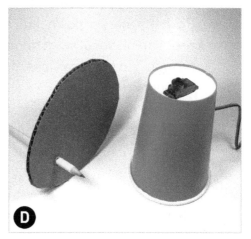

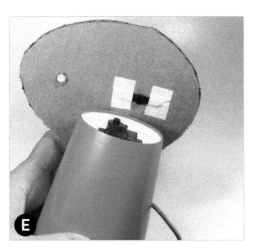

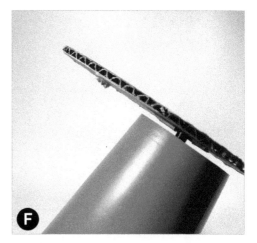

without making the robot tip over. If the holder tips your robot off-balance, move the servo horn to a better spot. (Another way to help balance it is to add some weight to the top; see the next step.)

3. To make the upper half of the robot body:
   - Take another cup, container, or other material and create an upper body and head to go on top of the marker holder. The example shows a cup that's been cut shorter (Figure **G**).
   - Put the marker back in, tip end down. Protect your work surface with some paper or cardboard, and remove the cap. (Put it on the other end of the marker if it fits.)
   - Push the marker down until it can draw on the paper. If it doesn't reach, think about ways to make the pen holder lower. (For instance, can you add more cardboard underneath the pen holder to make it thicker?)
   - When everything is working, check to see that the servo and the head are connected securely to the marker holder. Go back and add more tape if needed.

4. Next, connect the servo motor to the micro:bit, following the steps in the "**Servos and micro:bit**" box on page 163:

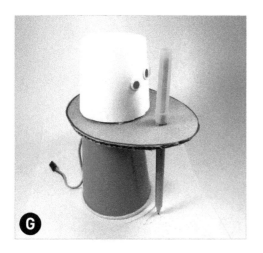

G

H

- Plug the servo cable wires into the alligator clip wires, matching the colors (Figure **H**).
- Clamp the alligator clip wires onto the micro:bit pins in this order (Figure **I**):
  - Brown or black – GND
  - Yellow or white – Pin 0
  - Orange or red – 3V
- To hold the wire ends together, you can wrap some masking tape around the plugs.

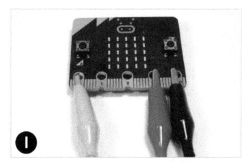

**I**

5. When you're finished building the body, you can decorate the robot however you choose. Color it, add stickers, glue on googly eyes, or use pipe cleaners for arms or hair (Figure **J**).

Now you're ready to code your robot!

**J**

# Servo Basics

A servo motor is different from regular motors because you can control how far and how fast it turns using computer programming. Mini servo motors are great for using with simple robots, because they can be controlled directly by small boards like the micro:bit. They're not very powerful, but they're perfect for lightweight designs made with paper and cardboard. (Bigger servos and regular motors need add-on hardware to work with microcontrollers.)

Just like regular motors, servos have a *shaft* — the part of the motor that sticks out and spins. To help you attach things to it, the servos you will use come with interchangeable *horns* — little plastic arms that snap onto the motor shaft. You usually get a variety of shapes with each servo. They all have tiny holes you can tie or hook things to, and come with a screw if you want to connect something to the servo more permanently.

There are two kinds of servo motors you may run into when building simple robots. For the projects in this book, you will be using *positional* servo motors. These motors can only turn halfway around, then pivot back. In robotics, they're used for heads, arms, legs, and other parts that need to swing back and forth. For spinning wheels or cranks, small robots use *continuous* servo motors, which look just like regular servo motors but can rotate all the way around. Make sure you are using the right kind of servo motor (and the right MakeCode blocks) for your robot!

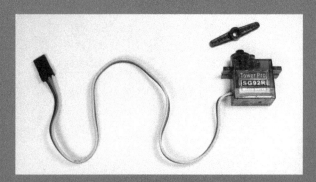

# Servos and micro:bit

To connect a servo to a board like micro:bit, you use its cable. The cable is made up of three wires in different colors:

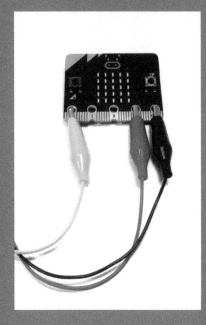

- **Orange or red is power.** It draws electricity from the micro:bit (or other source, such as a separate battery pack) to make the motor run.
- **Brown or black is ground.** It completes the circuit by bringing it back to the micro:bit.
- **Yellow or white is signal.** It carries the programming instructions from the micro:bit to the servo.

A connector at the end lets you plug wires into the servo cable. For the projects in this book, it's handy to use a connecting wire known as alligator-clip-to-male-header-pin. On one end, it has a pin that can plug into the servo cable. On

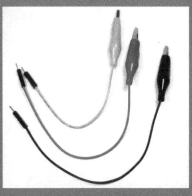

the other end, it has an alligator clip that can clamp onto the edge connector rings on the micro:bit. (To open the alligator clip, squeeze on its "head" and the "jaws" will open up. Let go, and they snap closed. The "teeth" will usually give you a good grip on the part you are connecting to.)

**It's very important to connect the wires from the servo to the correct pin on the micro:bit! You should also get used to attaching them in the correct order.** This will avoid damage to the servo or the micro:bit. If possible, use alligator clip wires that more-or-less match the colors of the servo cable wires. If not, attach little labels to each wire with tape to keep them straight. Here is how to attach them:

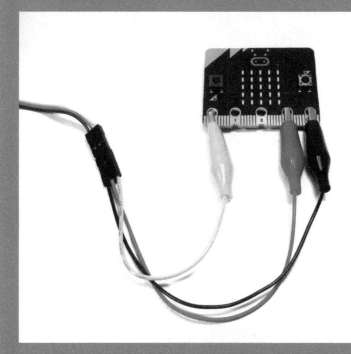

- **First:** Brown or black (ground) connects to the GND pin on the micro:bit.
- **Second:** Yellow or white (signal) gets connected to one of the micro:bit's three programmable pins, labeled as 0, 1, and 2. For the projects in this book, you'll connect the servo to Pin 0.
- **Third:** Orange or red (power) goes to the 3V pin. The name stands for "3 volts," which is the amount of power the micro:bit can send to another device.

# Servos and MakeCode

To program a servo motor with MakeCode, follow these steps:

1. MakeCode has special blocks to use with servos, but you have to add them to the list of categories. To find them:
   - Go to the bottom of the category list and click on "Advanced" (Figure 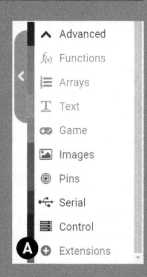A).
   - Scroll down to the bottom and click on "Extensions."
   - You'll jump to a new page, with many different extras you can add to MakeCode. Look for "servo" (with a green-and-blue drawing of a servo). Click on it and you will jump back to the MakeCode workpage (Figure B). The menu for Servos in dark green will appear in the middle of the other categories.

2. Open the Servos menu and drag the "set servo [P0] to [90] °" block to the workspace. Place it inside a block like "on start" to activate it (Figure C).

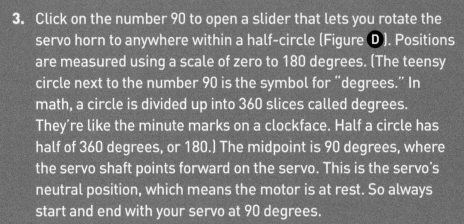

3. Click on the number 90 to open a slider that lets you rotate the servo horn to anywhere within a half-circle (Figure **D**). Positions are measured using a scale of zero to 180 degrees. (The teensy circle next to the number 90 is the symbol for "degrees." In math, a circle is divided up into 360 slices called degrees. They're like the minute marks on a clockface. Half a circle has half of 360 degrees, or 180.) The midpoint is 90 degrees, where the servo shaft points forward on the servo. This is the servo's neutral position, which means the motor is at rest. So always start and end with your servo at 90 degrees.

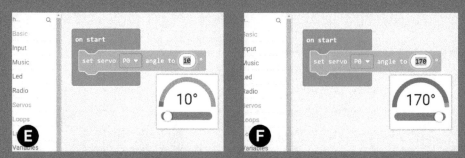

4. To move the servo to a different position, add more servo blocks to the stack, and change the position of the servo horn by using the slider or typing in the number of degrees. To avoid straining the little servo motor, don't make it go all the way to the ends. Limit its movement so it only goes between around 10 degrees and 170 degrees (Figures **E** and **F**).

5. To give the servo time to move before the program goes onto the next step, put a pause from the Basic menu (blue) after every

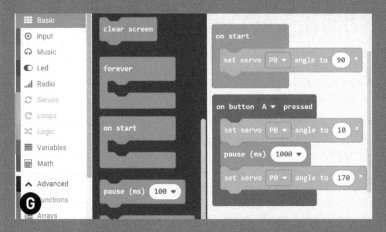

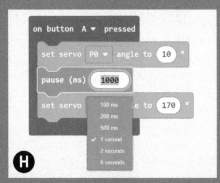

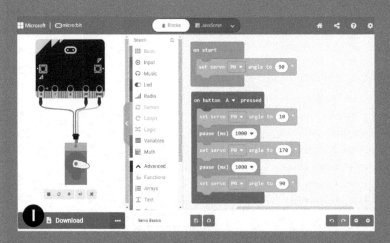

servo block (Figure G). Set the pause for around one second (1000 ms) (Figure H).

6. Remember to end with the servo at 90 degrees (Figure I). That's it!

# Accelerometer Basics

An accelerometer detects tilt and speed by comparing its readings to Earth's gravity. The pull of gravity on something sitting still on the Earth's surface is equal to 1g, which stands for "one gravity." When you move in any direction, you're adding to, or subtracting from, the pull of gravity, so the g-force goes up or down. On a micro:bit, the accelerometer measures forces in milli-gravities: 1,000mg equals 1g.

The micro:bit's accelerometer can also tell you which direction the movement is pointed in. Each direction is measured along an axis, like the kind used in graphs in math. The directions compared to the front of the micro:bit are:

- **x-axis:** tilt side to side
- **y-axis:** tilt forward and backward
- **z-axis:** up and down (compared to the floor)

On a graph, each axis is shown as a line, and all the lines cross in the middle. That point is zero on every axis. When you move to the top or to the right on the graph, or up towards the ceiling, the numbers get bigger (1, 2, 3 and so on). Move to the bottom, to the left, or down to the floor, and the numbers get smaller. They are negative numbers (-1, -2, -3, and so on) because they are less than zero.

For this project, you will be using readings along the x-axis in micro-gravities (mg). To show different amounts of tilt, the micro:bit translates those readings into numbers between -1023 (tilted all the way left) and 1023 (tilted all the way right). Zero is level (laying flat). You will have to take the micro:bit's number and translate it again, to degrees between 0 and 180 that the servo will understand. (See the "**Servo Basics**" box on page 162 for how that works.)

Why 1023 and -1023? Computers are basically a big collection of switches, which can be either on or off. To do their calculations, they use only two digits: 0 and 1. (That's called the *binary system*.) The micro:bit is a tiny computer that has a limited amount of memory, so the designers assigned $2^{10}$ (two multiplied by itself 10 times) for the accelerometer. That equals 1024, but since computers start counting at zero instead of one, you have to subtract one from 1024. The answer is 1023!

## INSTRUCTIONS FOR PROGRAMMING THE DRAWBOT WITH MAKECODE

To make your DrawBot scribble back and forth as it jiggles around, you will write code that turns the micro:bit board into a wired remote control. The micro:bit will use its built-in tilt sensor — known as an accelerometer — to tell the servo to swing to the right or the left, which will move the DrawBot's marker.

To practice working with sensors, you can try an easy version that simply moves the marker all the way left or all the way right. Then move on to the version that moves the marker different amounts, depending on how far the micro:bit is tilted. The program isn't very long, but it involves a new concept called *mapping*. Mapping lets you take the numbers that represent what the accelerometer measures and translate them into different numbers that tell the servo how far to turn. See the "**Accelerometer Basics**" box on page 168 for a quick explanation of how it works.

1. Begin by setting the servo in the neutral position:
   - Open the Servos menu (see the "**Servos and MakeCode**" box on page 165 for how to do that) and drag the "set servo [P0] to [90] °" block to the workspace.
   - Place it inside the "on start" block to activate it.

2. To write the easy version of the tilt-control remote control:
   - Drag an "on [shake]" block from the Input menu (light purple) into the workspace (Figure **A**).
   - Click on the little triangle-shaped down arrow to open the drop-down menu. Choose "tilt left" (Figure **B**).
   - Inside the "tilt left" block, put another "set servo" block. Open the slider and move it a bit to the left. How far will depend on the design of your DrawBot. You don't want to move the marker so much that the robot tips over. In the example here, the servo is set to 30 degrees (Figure **C**).
   - Add another servo block and return it to neutral (90 degrees). In between, add a pause block from the Basic menu (blue). Set it for 1 second (1,000 ms) (Figure **D**).

- To make the bot go right when the board is tilted the other way, you can just make a copy of the first stack of blocks and change the settings. Right click on the "tilt left" block to open a drop-down menu, and choose "Duplicate" (Figure **E**). Then change the copy to "tilt right" and move the servo to the other side (Figure **F**). The example here shows 150 degrees.
- Download the MakeCode to the board (see Chapter 4 if you need a refresher) and see if you like the way the bot works!

3. The advanced version of tilt control works a little differently. You have to take the measurements produced by the accelerometer and translate them into degrees the servo will turn. See the "**Accelerometer Basics**" box on page 168 for a quick explanation of how it works (Figure **G**).

4. Go to the Variables menu (red) to make a variable. Call it "angle." This variable will hold the number of degrees the servo shaft should turn. Then drag a "set [angle] to [0]" block inside a forever block (Figure **H**).

5. Below Advanced on the list of menus, find the Pins menu (brick red). Drag the fat oval "map [0]" block to the workspace. Insert it into the "set [angle]" block, right over the zero. Let it snap into place. Then change the values in the white openings on the "map [0]" (Figure **I**) block as follows:

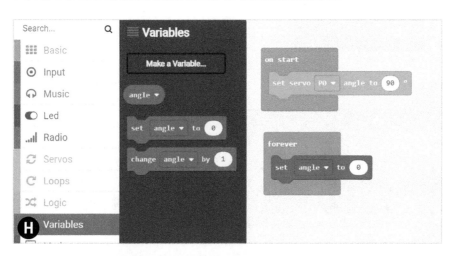

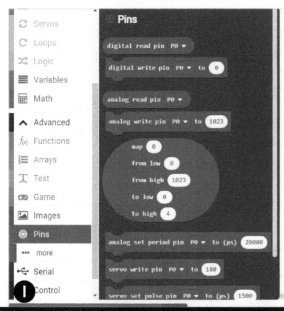

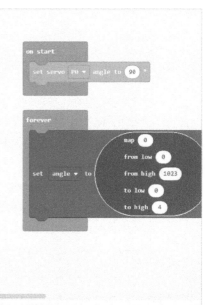

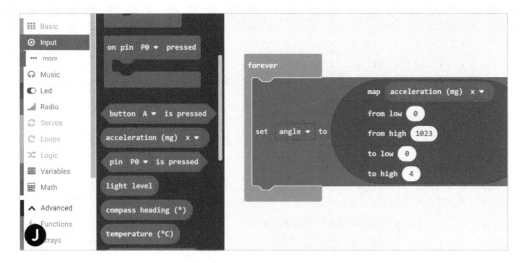

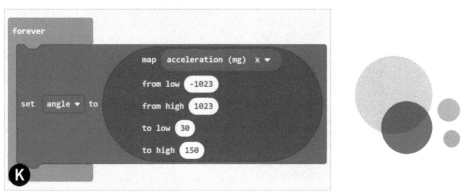

- Go to the Input menu and find the oval-shaped "acceleration (mg) [x]" block. Drag it over the first zero, next to "map," and let it snap into place (Figure **J**).
- The next two lines are the values from the accelerometer. Change "from low" to -1023. Don't forget the negative sign! Then change "from high" to 1023 (Figure **K**).
- The last two lines will translate the old low and high numbers to new ones. They will tell the servo to move to the left and right, but not all the way. Change "to low" to 30, and "to high" to 150. These are the numbers that worked best with the example DrawBot, but you can change them if your design is different.

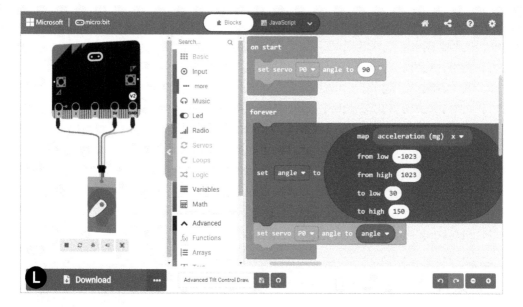

6. To finish this stack of blocks, drag a "set servo [P0] angle to [0]" block under the variable block inside the "forever" block. Replace the zero with an oval-shaped variable block that says "angle" (Figure **L**). You're ready to test it out!

   To see sample code using MakeCode tilt commands, go to Easy Tilt DrawBot: makecode.microbit.org/_TwE7ts3cD65A.

   To see sample MakeCode that uses a range of accelerometer readings to decide how far to move a pen, go to Advanced Tilt Control DrawBot: makecode.microbit.org/_g7q64A10aUD3.

## TROUBLESHOOTING TIPS

Here are some suggestions if the robot's body gives you problems:

- If the marker doesn't stay put in the holder, use masking tape or add extra cardboard to make the hole for the marker tighter.
- If the motor stops working, check that all the wires are still connected to the servo cable and the micro:bit in the correct order.

# GO BEYOND

- To add more markers, make a bigger marker holder.
  Poke holes for each marker in the holder, trying to keep
  the whole thing balanced so it doesn't tip over.
- To make arms that you can lengthen or shorten, cut strips of
  cardboard and connect them using brads (bendable metal paper
  holders that let you make movable joints). Attach two or more strips
  to make "scissor joints" that let the arms collapse and expand.
- With an extra micro:bit (or a different board, like the
  Adafruit Circuit Playground Express), you can use
  two servo motors to control scissor arms.

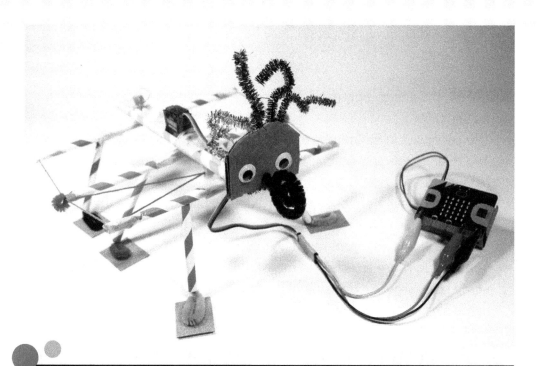

# Make a String Straw HexaWalker

**BUILD A JAUNTY LITTLE BUG-SHAPED ROBOT THAT USES ONLY ONE SERVO TO MOVE ALL SIX LEGS!**

As humans, most of the creatures we hang out with have two (or four!) legs. But get down to ground level, or take a look at what's buzzing around your head, and six legs seems to be the way to go, as far as Nature is concerned. That extra pair of legs makes a body more stable, without requiring a lot more brain power. It explains why hexapods — robotic walkers with six legs — are enormously popular as toys, research designs, and homemade robots. Many robots with whegs, like those in Chapter 2, have six (or more!) wheel legs.

Hexapod robots use different **gaits**, or patterns of walking, depending on how they are designed and how many servos they use. The gait determines which legs move forward or backward (or up and down) at which times.

The hexapod design you will build here has front and back legs that move together, and middle legs that move in the opposite direction.

Best of all, the design only needs one servo to make all the legs move! It works like this:

- The servo sits in the middle of the body, upside down.
- The middle legs are attached directly to the servo, and pivot forward and back.
- The front legs are attached to the middle legs with strings that cross. When one side of the middle legs moves back, the string pulls the opposite side of the front legs back at the same time.
- The front legs are attached to the back legs by strings on the same side. So when one side of the front legs pivots forward, it pulls the same side of the back legs forward at the same time.

The illustration below shows you how the strings are connected to the legs. If it seems complicated, it will make more sense when you build it!

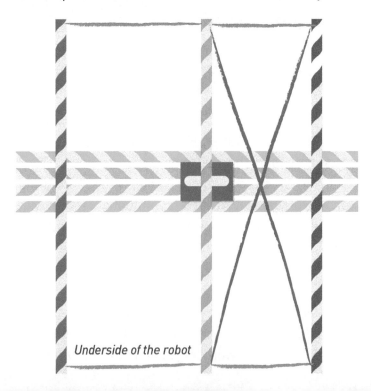

*Underside of the robot*

## WHAT TO EXPECT

- **Time Needed:** 1 hour
- **Cost:** $25–$30 (including re-usable electronics)
- **Difficulty:** Moderate
- **Safety Issues:** Use care with electronics and batteries, especially with younger children.

## SKILLS YOU WILL USE

- Learning different ways to connect a micro:bit to a robot
- Using strings as actuators (components that move parts of a robot)
- Testing and improving the design of a robot

## ELECTRONIC SUPPLIES

- micro:bit V2 microcontroller (v1 will also work, but won't include sound)
- USB data cable with a USB micro-B plug and an end that fits your computer
- Micro servo (positional, not continuous) — often labeled as 9g
  - a cable with a plug that takes male jumper wires
  - a servo horn with 4 arms — at least two of them long
- 3 alligator clip-to-male jumper wires in different colors (preferably red, black or brown, and yellow or orange to match the servo wires)
- Optional:
  - extra-long USB data cable (3 feet or more), so your bot can move around while connected to the computer for power and updating the program
  - additional male-to-female jumper wires for longer distance remote control
  - battery pack for the micro:bit

    the punch-out cardboard battery pack holder that comes with some micro:bits is handy for holding the board and batteries together; print and cut out your own from the micro:bit site (microbit.org/get-started/user-guide/battery-pack-holder).

    you can also get a larger pack that holds two AA batteries and has an on/off switch

## CRAFT SUPPLIES

If you don't have any of these materials on hand, try substituting what you've got!

- 9 paper straws
- 3 pipe cleaners
- Twist-tie wire (comes in rolls for gardening)
- Masking tape
- 4 pony beads (or other large, lightweight beads with big holes)
- Embroidery yarn (cotton)
- Paperboard (flat cardboard with at least one rough side)
- Optional: supplies to make a "face" for the robot, such as corrugated cardboard, extra pipe cleaners, and googly eyes
- Pencil (for marking lengths and poking holes — a ball point pen or bamboo skewer are good for holes too)
- Scissors

## INSTRUCTIONS FOR BUILDING THE BODY AND CONNECTING THE ELECTRONICS

To make the body, including a hole for the servo motor:

1. Take two straws and cut them in half. Arrange the straws side by side, with the cut edges facing out.
   - Place two more straws on either side of the cut straws, lining up the ends.
   - Spread the cut halves apart to leave a gap of about 3/4 inch (2 centimeters). Take the servo and test that it can fit in the gap snugly (Figure **A**).
   - Wrap masking tape around all four straws at the edge of the gap in the middle and at the ends. Keep the straws flat, like a raft.

2. To attach the servo motor to the body:
   - Turn the servo upside down and insert it into the gap in the middle of the body. The "shoulders" of the servo should be sitting on the straws. The cable for the servo faces the front of the body (so you

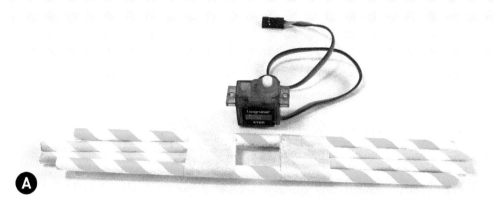

A

have the option to attach the micro:bit to the robot's "face") (Figure **B**).

- Use masking tape to hold the servo in place.

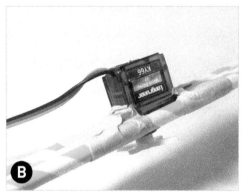

B

3. To start the legs and feet:
   - Take three straws. Insert pipe cleaners inside each straw, with the ends sticking out of the straws evenly (Figure **C**).
   - With a pencil or pen, make marks 2 1/2 inches (6 centimeters) from each end of the straw (or however long you want the legs to be). Take something with a flat edge, like round-tipped scissors, a flat screwdriver, or the end of a spoon. Press down at the marks to bend the straw and make the legs pop up (Figure **D**). Make sure to bend each side of the straw in the same direction

C

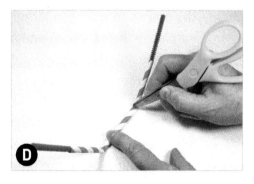

D

**E**

**F**

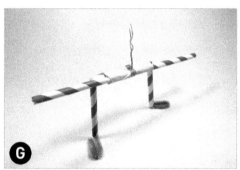

**G**

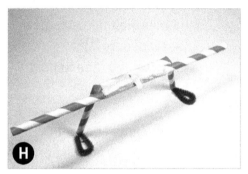

**H**

so that the legs face the same way.
- Curve the ends of the pipe cleaners around to make feet (Figure **E**).

4. To finish the legs:
   - Take three more straws. Make a mark in the middle of each straw.
   - Cut three pieces of twist tie wire about 8 inches (20 centimeters) long. Set one piece of wire aside for now.
   - On two of the straws, wrap a piece of wire tightly around the middle of the straw, leaving a couple inches of wire loose at each end. Twist the ends of the wire together to tighten up the wrapped part of the wire so it can't slide up and down the straw (Figure **F**).
   - Take one set of legs and hold it next to one of the straws with the wire. The feet should face towards the straw with the wire. Wrap masking tape around both straws on either side of the wrapped wire to hold the straws tightly together (Figure **G**). Repeat with a second set of legs.
   - Take the third straw and tape the servo horn on in the middle. The

servo should face up so it can attach to the servo. (Make sure not to tape over the opening that fits over the servo shaft.) Then attach it to the remaining set of legs (Figure **H**).

5.  To attach the middle legs to the body:
    *   Press the servo horn onto the servo shaft. Make sure the feet are facing front. Test that the legs can pivot right and left by *gently* holding onto it near the servo horn and turning it like a dial.
    *   To make sure the servo shaft is pointing the right way:
        *   *Gently* turn the legs as far to the right as they will go. The legs should be facing all the way to the right as well. If they are not, pull the servo horn and the legs off, and put them back on in the correct position.
        *   Then *gently* turn the legs, still connected to the servo motor, so they face the front.
        *   You may want to remove the middle legs while you attach the front and back legs. If you do, just pop them back on, facing front.

6.  To attach the front and rear legs to the body:
    *   At the back end of the body, use the point of a pencil to make a hole for the wire between the middle two straws.
    *   Insert the wires of the rear legs up through the hole. Make sure the feet face the front of the body (Figure **I**)! (The servo cable will also face the front.)
    *   Spread the wires to the sides, pulling the legs up close to the underside of the body. Make sure the legs can pivot right and left.
    *   Bend the wires back towards each other. Where they meet, bend the wires again so they are pointing up. This

will make a little tab on each side to help keep the wires from sliding back down through the hole.

- Slide a bead over the ends of the wires and press it down as far as it will go. Bend the remaining wire around the sides of the bead to hold it in place. Don't trim any extra wire yet (Figure **J**).
- Repeat with the front legs at the front end of the robot. Again, make sure the feet face front. Also make sure the legs can turn smoothly to the right and left.
- Make sure the robot can stand on its own six feet before going on. The middle legs may be a little longer than the front and back legs. You can adjust this by changing the angle of the legs, or make the pipe cleaner feet higher or lower. Don't worry too much — you can adjust the length of the legs again later if needed (Figure **K**).

**IMPORTANT:** For this step, make sure the legs always face front and line up parallel to each other!

7. Next, attach the string or yarn to make the front legs move.
   - To hold the string, insert your scissors into the end of each straw and cut two little slots in the sides (Figure **L**).
   - Cut four pieces of yarn about 14 inches (35 centimeters) long. Two will cross in the front, and two will go along the sides. Tie a knot in one end of each piece of yarn, about 1/2 inch (1 centimeter) from the end (Figure **M**).

- Take one of the strings and slide it into the slot on the left side of the middle legs. Pull gently until the knot rests up against the outside of the straw (Figure **N**).
- Slide a bead onto the yarn. Then pull the other end over the right side of the front legs. Insert the yarn into the slot on that end of the straw. Pull the yarn until it is tight. (Are the legs still facing the front? Good!) Tie a knot on the other end of the yarn. Try to get it close to the outside of the front straw, but don't worry if it's not exact. You will tape it in place later (Figure **O**).

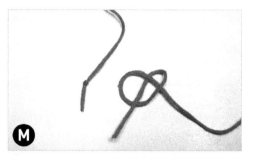

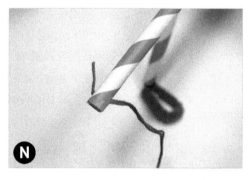

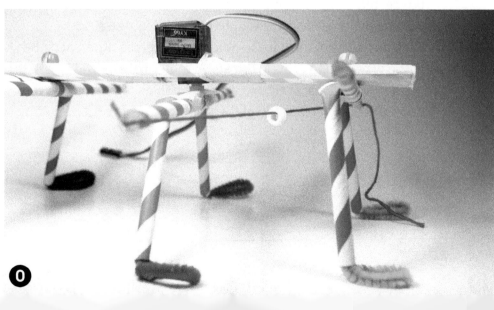

P

- Repeat with another piece of yarn, going from the right side of the middle legs to the left side of the front legs. Insert the yarn through the same bead as the first piece (Figure **P**).
- To hold the bead in place:
  - Take the third piece of wire you cut in Step 4 and insert it through the bead. Give it a twist to hold it in place (Figure **Q**).
  - Insert the ends of the wire through another bead, on top of the first bead. The hole of the second bead will be facing up and down (Figure **R**).
  - Poke a hole between the two middle straws on the body with a pencil, the same way you did for the front and back legs. Insert the ends of the wire up through the hole (Figure **S**).
  - Twist the ends of the wire to hold them in place. Run each end of the wire up and around the servo motor cables, and twist the remaining wire securely on top of the cables. Do the same with the remaining wire on top of the front legs (Figure **T**).

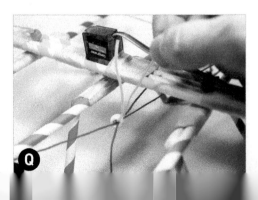

Q

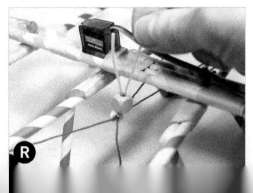

R

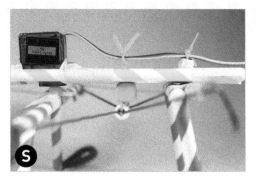

8. To connect the front and rear legs:
   - Insert a string into the slot on the left side of the rear legs, the same way you did for the middle legs. Bring it up along the side and slide the other end into the left side of the front legs. Make the string tight (keep those legs facing front!) and knot the other end. Repeat with the right side of the front and rear legs.
   - To make a loop to hold the side strings in place:
     - Cut two pieces of pipe cleaner, about 3 inches (8 centimeters) long. Curve the ends up so they meet, then bend down a little bit at the ends (Figure **U**).
     - Put one loop of pipe cleaner over one of the side strings. Squeeze the ends of the loop together tightly and insert them into one end of the middle straw. Leave enough of the loop sticking out to allow the string to slide through it easily. Repeat with the other piece of pipe cleaner on the other side (Figure **V**).

9. Test that your legs move as they are supposed to by again *gently* turning

the middle legs side to side, as you did before. **If one of the strings doesn't slide smoothly, do not force it!** This could put strain on the servo motor and damage it. When everything is working, secure the ends of the strings to the straws with masking tape.

10. The last step is to attach "shoes" to the feet. These will help the feet stay flat, and add a little weight that helps them move (Figure **W**). To make the shoes:

    • Cut some thin cardboard into six pieces. In the example here, the shoes are about an inch (2 centimeters) long and a little less wide. You can make yours any shape you want.

    • Tape the pipe cleaner feet onto the paperboard shoes.

    • Adjust the feet so they are flat on the walking surface. If possible, make all the legs tilt back a little. You can adjust them when you fire up the motor and see how they walk!

11. Connect the micro:bit to the servo as you did before (Figure **X**) (see the **"Servo Basics"** box on page 162). You're ready to code!

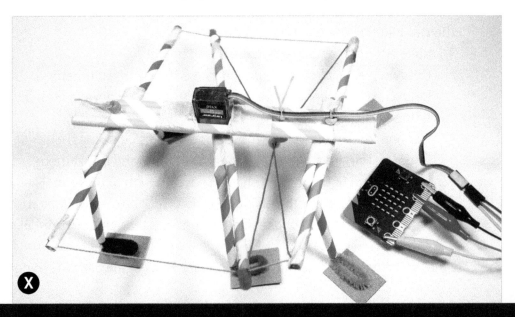

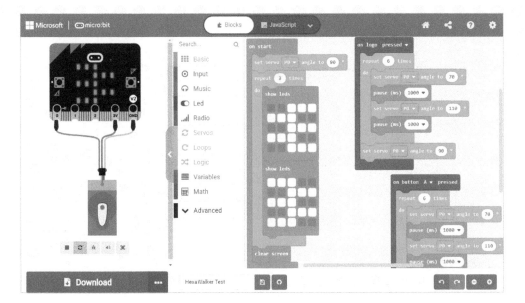

## INSTRUCTIONS FOR PROGRAMMING THE HEXAWALKER WITH MAKECODE

If you've already tried out MakeCode with the earlier projects in this book, then this program should be super easy. (If you haven't, go back and read the "**Servos and MakeCode**" box on page 165.) This sample code is designed to let you test your HexaWalker while it is still plugged into your computer with a USB cable. That way, you can quickly make adjustments based on your tests.

1. In the "on start" block, insert a "set servo" block to put the servo at the 90-degree neutral position.

2. You may want to add some light animation or sound so you know your program is running when the micro:bit starts up. In this example, the LED grid will flash an animation that looks like a bug scrambling away.

3. To make the robot move:
   - When the micro:bit is plugged into the computer, you will need to hold the board and the USB cable while the robot walks. So pick an input that's easy to reach. If you've got the micro:bit v2, you can use the logo

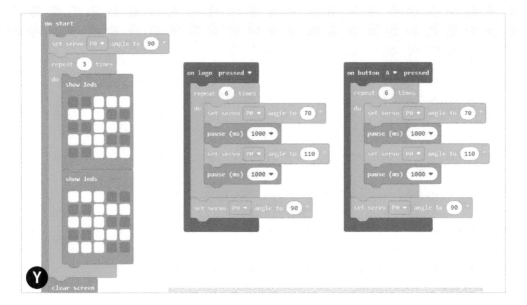

press block. (The little brass-colored face at the top of the micro:bit is the logo touch sensor.) If you're using the original version, use the "on button [A] pressed" input block instead (Figure **Y**).

- For this hexapod design, the servo doesn't have to move far to swing the legs back and forth. The exact distance to set the servo to move will depend on your model. To test it out, start by setting the servo to swing to 70 degrees (a little to the left of neutral) and then to 110 degrees (a little to the right of neutral).
- Add a pause of 1 second (1000 ms) after each movement of the servo. Then place a repeat block around this stack of code to make the servo swing back and forth several times. In the example shown above, it's set to repeat six times.
- After the repeat, add one more block to set the servo back to neutral (90).

4. To test your code with your HexaWalker:
   - Make sure the alligator clip wires are attached to your micro:bit and to the servo motor cable in the correct order. You can wrap some masking tape around the wires' plugs to hold them in place.
   - Download the MakeCode to the micro:bit.

- Put your HexaWalker on a flat surface. Make sure the feet are flat. Hold the micro:bit and the cables out of the way of the robot. Touch the logo (or push the button) and see if the robot goes!
- If the robot barely moves, try changing the code to make the servo swing a little further in each direction. Click on the angle number to open the slider that shows where the servo angle is. You will make the first servo number smaller and the second servo number bigger.
- If the servo is making the middle legs swing too far, and they are bumping into the other legs or getting tangled up, try shortening the distance the servo swings.
- When you find the right settings, the HexaWalker should stroll along with a happy gait!

To see sample code, go to HexaWalker Test makecode.microbit.org/_95aEFhJjt7V4.

## GO BEYOND
- Free your HexaWalker from the computer by plugging in the micro:bit's battery pack holder. Use the punch-out cardboard holder that comes with some micro:bits, or print and cut out your own from the micro:bit site (microbit.org/get-started/user-guide/battery-pack-holder).
- Make a face for your robot. One suggestion is to insert pipe cleaners inside the tunnels in a piece of corrugated cardboard. Bend the bottoms and insert them in the straws that make up the body. Bend the tops however you like. You also have room for googly eyes or whatever else you'd like to add.
- Instead of a logo or button press, code your robot to respond to loud sounds (like the FiberBot in Chapter 4) or changes in light.

# Invent Your Own Hexapod Robot

There are lots of different ways to build a hexapod robot — even one that uses only a single servo motor. The version in these instructions took many *iterations* (tries) to get it to look and work the way I planned. Want to try designing your own? Here are some of the things you'll need to think about:

- **The body:** What shape will you make it? What kind of materials will you use? And how can you keep it all light enough to avoid straining the motor?

- **The legs:** Will you make them shorter or taller? Straight up and down, spreading out to the sides, or leaning back? What shape feet might you add?

- **The servo motor:** What happens if you move it to the front or the back? What if it sits on top instead of underneath the body?

- **String, wire, tape, and other connectors:** Is there a better way to string the robot up? What can you use in place of masking tape to make your robot hold together more permanently?

- **The electronic brain and the programmable body:** How can the code be improved? What else can you make the robot do? For instance, can you make the robot dance, or walk backwards?

# HOPE YOU HAD FUN MAKING SIMPLE ROBOTS!
## WHAT WILL YOU CREATE NEXT? IT'S UP TO YOU!

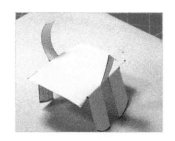

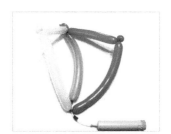

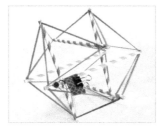
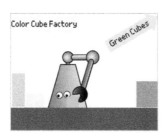

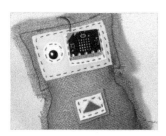

## ABOUT THE AUTHOR

**Kathy Ceceri** is an award-winning writer, educator, and maker, with a focus on science, technology, history, and art. The author of over a dozen books for kids featuring hands-on STEAM activities, Kathy teaches enrichment workshops at schools, museums, libraries, and afterschool programs, both in person and online. She also works with educators and parents looking for ways to make learning more engaging and fun. In addition, Kathy develops teaching and learning materials for companies like Make: Community and Adafruit Industries, as well as organizations including the Girl Scouts of the USA, where she helped design a series of robotics badges and a nationwide cybersecurity competition. Kathy lives along the Hudson River in Upstate New York.

# Index

## A

accelerometer, 116, 134, 168-170, 172, 174, 175
actuators, 179
Adafruit Industries, 176, 195
adhesive dots, 44
Ai-Da, 151
air muscles, 19, 23
Alexa, 68
algorithm, 74, 87, 93, 99, 132
Ameca, 108
artificial intelligence (AI), 68
automata, 153

## B

batteries, 30, 117, 118, 127, 156, 157, 179
Baymax, 18
BEAM, 151, 152
biomimetic, 1, 9
Block Palette (Scratch), 71-73, 83
Boston Dynamics, 4
Breazeal, Cynthia, 104

## C

C-3PO, 103
CAD software, 51
    Tinkercad, 51-65
Case Western Reserve University, 27
Chibitronics, 29
circuits, 30-33, 41, 47, 49, 67
Circuit Stickers, 29
conditional commands, 67, 73

conductive, 30, 33, 41, 44, 47, 49, 149
copper tape, 47, 48
Cornell University, 8
Crayola Model Magic, 109
cyborg, 114, 115

## D

Diana, Carla, 104
dimmer switch, 50

## E

Eliza (chatbot), 67-70, 74
Engineered Arts, 108, 151

## F

Felt, Wyatt, 19
Festo, 9, 10, 17
FiberBot, 114-149
foil tape, 33, 38
Franklin Institute, 154
Fuller, Buckminster, 42

## G

gaits, 4, 177
Geminoid (Osaka University), 108
Glue dots, 157
Griffith, Saul, 19
Guitar Touch Tunes, 149

## H

Hanson Robotics, 107
Hanson, David, 107, 108
Hexawalker, 152, 177-192
Hexbug, 27, 152

MakeCode, 105, 115, 118, 128-130, 132, 133, 138, 139, 144, 156, 162,
    165, 169, 170, 172, 175, 189-191
mapping, 170
Marty (robot), 115
McKibben, Joseph L., 19
Meller, Aidan, 151
MGonz (chatbot), 69, 70
micro:bit, 105, 115-149, 155, 156, 160-176
Minecraft, 52
MIT Media Labs Personal Robots Group, 104
Mitsuku (chatbot), 70
Mori, Masahiro, 106, 108
motors, 27, 43, 152, 162, 163
motorized, 25, 30, 31, 44, 47-50, 65, 67, 155, 158, 160, 165, 166, 175, 176,
    180, 183, 186, 188, 190, 192

## N
NASA Ames Research Center, 28

## O
octopus, 1, 9
origami, 29
origami robot, 32-41
Osaka University, 108
OtherLab, 19

## P
PancakeBot, 155
Pandorabots, 70
Paro (robot), 115
passive dynamic walking, 3, 4, 8
Pettis, Bre, 43
Philip K. Dick, 107
pick-and-place, 84, 103

CPSIA information can be obtained
at www.ICGtesting.com
Printed in the USA
BVHW010517290422
635633BV00001BA/1

9 781680 457308